Helping the Homeless

Helping the Homeless

Where Do We Go from Here?

John R. Belcher
Frederick A. DiBlasio

Lexington Books
D.C. Heath and Company/Lexington, Massachusetts/Toronto

Library of Congress Cataloging-in-Publication Data

Belcher, John R.
  Helping the homeless : where do we go from here? / John R.
Belcher, Frederick A. DiBlasio.
    p.   cm.
    ISBN 0–669–21523–6. — ISBN 0–669–21522–8 (pbk.)
    1. Homelessness—United States. I. DiBlasio, Frederick A.
II. Title.
HV4505.B46   1990
363.5'0973—dc20   89–26826
                                    CIP

Published simultaneously in Canada
Printed in the United States of America
Casebound International Standard Book Number: 0–669–21523–6
Library of Congress Catalog Card Number: 89–26826

The paper used in this publication meets the minimum requirements of
American National Standard for Information Sciences—Permanence of
Paper for Printed Library Materials, ANSI Z39.48–1984. ∞™

The first and last numbers below indicate year and number of printing.

90 91 92 10 9 8 7 6 5 4 3 2 1

Contents

Tables

Preface

Much of the discussion that has taken place concerning homelessness has focused on documenting the plight of the homeless and advocating the development of more shelters and soup kitchens. We have decided to approach the problem differently. In this book we examine how people become homeless and offer potential solutions for helping prevent people from becoming homeless and also for helping those who are already homeless escape their plight.

It is our contention that much homelessness results from economic dislocation. We define *economic dislocation* as a process in which individuals are adversely affected by the U.S. economic system. For some, this could mean job loss as the result of a leveraged buy-out. For others, it could mean neglect by government agencies charged with their care. Therefore, we focus on changes in the economic system that will enable the United States to provide more stable opportunities to its citizens.

Chapter 1 examines the deindustrialization of the United States and the new-style corporate philosophy that has resulted in dramatic changes for a growing segment of the work force. Homelessness is no longer an accident for many individuals; instead, it results from corporate and government approaches to the management of the economy.

In chapter 2 we review some of our work that led to the hypothesis of economic dislocation. Surprisingly, we found that many homeless individuals work but are unable to avoid homelessness. We develop implications for designing research models that can be used to examine more closely the phenomenon of economic dislocation.

In chapter 3 we develop options for resolving the homeless crisis. In our view the U.S. market system is in need of both planned revitilization and government oversight. We suggest methods by which the economy can achieve renewed growth and at the same time *not* further expose working individuals to the negative consequences of economic dislocation.

Chapter 4 focuses on needed changes in the nation's education system so that future workers will be adequately prepared for the shifting job market.

Otherwise, as the economy is restructured, more Americans will be unable to find jobs and will become homeless.

In chapter 5 we explore the housing crisis and suggest that a new mix of public and private housing alternatives needs to be offered. Much of the housing crisis has been created by the particular financing schemes used, and we suggest a more heavily concentrated government effort in this area to prevent abuses.

Many of the homeless have been observed to be mentally ill. Chapter 6 offers ways to help prevent the mentally ill from becoming homeless.

Similarly, many of the homeless have been observed to abuse alcohol. In chapter 7 Drs. Brent B. Benda and Elizabeth D. Hutchison examine the prevalence of alcohol abuse among the homeless and offer ways to reduce the incidence of alcohol abuse.

Finally, chapter 8 explores the problem of homelessness in a global context. It would be too easy for us to offer solutions for the United States and ignore how these policies affect homelessness in other countries. Unfortunately, there is no easy answer to homelessness when a global backdrop is used to gauge potential solutions.

Our book is a series of options, for in the final analysis, helping the homeless requires us as a nation to make some hard choices. The homelessness crisis is too great and too intertwined with our socio-educational-political-economic system to ignore. Difficult and painful choices must be made in order to resolve the problem. Otherwise, homelessness will continue to grow, causing great human suffering and adding to the deterioration of our nation's productive capacity.

Acknowledgments

We would like to thank the following people for their help in reviewing the manuscript, making suggestions, and editing copy: Noreen Honeycutt, Steve Staley, Patti Davis-Belcher, and Michael Campbell. In addition, we would like to thank our wives, Patti and Jean, along with our families for their support and for listening to our ideas.

1
From Where Did They Come?

G overnment officials, the public, and social scientists are becoming increasingly aware of the need to do something about the homeless. Some people think the problem has reached epidemic proportions, requiring urgent changes in housing and welfare policies. Others, however, continue to rely on the belief that charity will resolve the crisis. For them, the solution is to build more shelters and open more soup kitchens. Still others would prefer to ignore the homeless, hoping that they will somehow disappear. These officials believe that economic policies in effect today will eventually allow prosperity to trickle down to the poorest of the poor.

These various positions overlook the notion that structures of society, such as government and business, have created an environment in which homelessness is a likely situation for an increasing number of Americans. Of course, business people and government officials have not conspired to create homelessness; instead, society simply is indifferent to the consequences of everyday business and government decision making. Solutions currently proposed by government leaders fail to address the causes of homelessness. If the cause of the problem is not addressed in the solution, the solution is doomed. This chapter focuses on one major cause of homelessness: economic dislocation.

Economic dislocation is a process that begins with an event caused by a factor in the economic system. For example, a person with an alcohol problem may loose his or her job. Why did this take place? We contend that economic factors have a bearing on the decision of an employer to fire or lay off the worker who is an alcohol abuser. In a labor market where workers are scarce, the employer may not fire the worker. On the other hand, in a labor market where there are many individuals looking for work, the employer may fire the worker. Throughout this chapter we will examine how economic factors impact on workers and often lead to a chain of events that frequently results in a loss of resources and supports for the worker. It is this process of loss triggered by an economic situation that we refer to as *economic dislocation*.

Public policy has seldom been able to address the needs of those individuals who are not able, either temporarily or permanently, to succeed in the economic mainstream. Instead, public policy makers are much more adept at blaming the victim. Homeless people are particularly difficult to understand because they represent an anomaly in an era of relatively low unemployment rates and economic prosperity. Not surprisingly, most Americans have difficulty conceptualizing the homeless as not being at fault for their condition. As a result, politicians and human service professionals have nurtured a belief that the homeless simply need a helping hand or a sympathetic ear.

Against this backdrop of blaming the victim, we are concerned with the origins of the homeless crisis. How did America arrive at a point in its history in which homelessness has become commonplace? This concern will be the focus of this chapter. It is our contention that effective public policy will not move forward in addressing the needs of this population until these issues are examined.

Who Are the Homeless?

To an untrained observer, the homeless appear to be characterized by a high percentage of mentally ill individuals. Interestingly, because of difficulties in counting the homeless and determining their total population, it is impossible to definitively say how many of the homeless are chronically mentally ill. Methods for counting the homeless invariably attempt to project, on the basis of a randomized sample, the approximate number of homeless people. However, since researchers cannot agree on a definition of what types of shelter conditions should be defined as homeless, the sample is usually very narrowly defined as those individuals who are living in the streets or in actual homeless shelters. This definition, however, overlooks those individuals who are living with family or friends on a temporary basis. Even when consensus is reached on a definition, it is difficult to locate and interview homeless people because of their tendency to wander and, of course, their lack of a specific place they call their own.

Homeless people can also be found in other living situations. Jails are frequently home, at least temporarily, to individuals who are homeless and are arrested for a crime, such as disturbing the peace. Finally, many mentally ill individuals who are temporarily hospitalized are homeless. They were homeless when admitted and, because of inadequate support systems, will become homeless upon discharge, so it makes sense to consider these individuals as homeless. However, these groups are generally not included among counts of the homeless. As a result, estimates of the number of homeless people within a city or even nationwide have varied widely.

Also important to consider when evaluating counts of the homeless is the agency or group of researchers performing the counting. For example, in 1984, the U.S. Department of Housing estimated the total number of homeless people nationwide at somewhere around 300,000 (Rich 1988). However, advocates for the homeless have estimated the number at around 3 million. Why the dramatic difference? Government officials may want low estimates because a high number of homeless people could prove costly to overburdened social service programs and cast doubt about the effectiveness of our economy to raise people out of poverty. On the other hand, advocates for the homeless want their counts to reflect the desperate nature of a homeless existence.

In addition to the mentally ill, the homeless include teenagers who have run away from home, substance abusers who involuntarily or voluntarily left employment, victims of family violence, the unemployed, the unemployable (such as handicapped people), and those who suffer some misfortune such as an apartment fire and lack adequate resources to sustain a loss. Among these individuals are victims of economic dislocation, some of them manifesting deviant behaviors such as substance abuse. Researchers have been quick to note the high incidence of these behaviors and consider them major contributors to homelessness. As a result, social scientists seldom explore the role of economic dislocation as a contributor to homelessness.

The vast majority of the studies on homeless people have not attempted to typologize them into categories that are characteristic of their pathways into homelessness. Exceptions include those studies that have examined types of psychiatric diagnoses and how individuals become homeless (Arce et al. 1983; Belcher & Toomey 1988). Other studies have examined the availability of resources (Rooney 1980) as a possible pathway into homelessness. Most studies, however, have examined the problem as if the reasons people become homeless had to do with individual failings (Perr 1985; Farr 1984).

Rather than explore the chain of events or the circumstances in homeless peoples' lives that may have contributed to their current situation, these researchers appear to be content with simply noting those behaviors that can be most easily observed and measured, such as alcohol abuse. As a result, homelessness is ascribed to behavioral problems, and the circumstances that created the behaviors, such as economic dislocation, are not explored. It is our contention that behaviors are frequently symptoms of frustration, anger, depression, and hopelessness. Rather than focus on the reactions to these problems, we choose to focus on the underlying causes.

Milburn & Watts (1985–86) reviewed the conceptual frameworks used to understand the problem. Interestingly, these researchers did not note a major flaw: a failure to examine the changing economic context in America. Some studies (Segal et al. 1977; Wallace 1968) have noted social disruption as contributing to homelessness, but the fact that economic dislocation created much of this social disruption has been overlooked or minimized. In fact, Milburn and Watts have urged researchers to maintain the status quo by exploring the relationship between types of homeless people and the kinds of resources they use. This focus will shed little light on how they became homeless. In a sense, homelessness has been conceptualized and studied as if it occurred in a vacuum.

The notion that the structures of society are sound and that it is the individual failings of people that cause social problems provides government with a justifiable rationale for conducting business as usual (Murray 1984; Anderson 1978). Many researchers, particularly in biomedicine, psychiatry, and psychology, have developed further justification for the individual deficit hypothesis, concluding that many of the homeless who abuse alcohol have lived lives in which their alcoholism was a major contributor to their homelessness (Karno et al. 1987). Illustrative of this method of inquiry is a study conducted in Baltimore that found that many individuals among the homeless population surveyed were alcoholics. These individuals also were more likely to come from families in which both parents had a drinking problem (Fischer et al. 1986). This association, while perhaps interesting, does not identify how alcohol contributed to homelessness. Studies have confirmed that adult children from alcoholic families often manifest problems of various types. Nevertheless, the contextual background of these problems, such as economic conditions, has not been adequately explored. As already noted, during relatively good economic times, a company may overlook troublesome behaviors that result from drinking. However, when the company experiences an economic downturn, the worker with an alcohol problem is generally the first to go.

Another way to understand troublesome behavior that results from alcohol abuse is to view it as reflective of desperate people with little hope for the future. Their frustration, depression, and anger are responses to their hopelessness. Wilson (1987) describes many of the poor, particularly the urban underclass, as:

> . . . living in neighborhoods characterized by long-term poverty, joblessness, high percentages of unwed mothers, high rates of welfare dependency, and various expressions of social pathology such as adolescent parenting, high school dropouts, drug abuse, and crime. (p. 55)

This view of pathological behaviors does not ignore the prospect that biological factors play a role in the development of mental illness. In fact, stress-vulnerability models of mental illness are based on the notion that noxious elements in the environment, such as economic deprivation, can exacerbate and set into motion mental health problems.

Wilson's analysis of the human condition also highlights how economic deprivation can create frustration, anger, and hopelessness, which in turn can be defined as mental illness by policy makers and society. In other words, in addition to those individuals with a vulnerability toward certain types of mental illness, there are individuals who, because of their desperate living conditions, will develop problems that can be defined as mental illness. It is economic deprivation, Wilson argues, that set in motion the chain of events that created an environment ripe for the development of mental health problems. While scholars attempt to project the amount of mental health problems within these poverty-stricken neighborhoods, a focus on estimating the connection between economic deprivation and homelessness is overlooked.

Although shelter surveys have provided some information about those individuals who frequent shelters, the problems of those people who temporarily live with family or friends is ignored. Certainly, those on the street are homeless. Those who live with family or friends on a temporary basis, who have no other home in which to return, and who are uncertain about where they will obtain their next week's lodging are also homeless. This latter description of homelessness, however, raises concerns that the current percentage of the Gross National Product (GNP) being expended on programs for special interests and the wealthy might have to be re-examined. It has long been argued by social activists that the affluent receive the lion's share of government subsidies and the poor receive as little as politically possible. Often what little the poor do receive is criticized as excessive. In fact, David Stockman (1986), former director of President Reagan's Office of Management and Budget, labeled the Reagan Revolution as a "frontal assault" on the welfare state.

The attack on the welfare state is also a priority of President Bush, who is positioning his forces in an effort to reduce the capital gains tax. Meanwhile, a minimum wage bill, which would have benefited the working poor, was vetoed. Admittedly, there is only so much GNP or output in this nation. As a result, competing interest groups attempt to ensure that they get their piece of the pie. Politicians have found it difficult to take benefits or money away from vocal interest groups such as the middle class, developers, retired citizens, or major corporations. The poor, however, rarely vote and do not generally advocate for their self-interest. Therefore, the way society defines poverty and what group is worthy of government support is as much a political process as it is a scholarly exercise. A broader definition of poverty poses difficulties to policy makers attempting to frame the problem as resulting solely from individual failings.

As a result, there is a dearth of information documenting the fact that many of the homeless are victims of economic dislocation. The homeless are viewed as primarily in need of more shelters and increased emergency health and mental health services. Voluntarism also is put forth as a method for addressing the needs of the homeless. All these approaches, however, are based on the assumption that the structures of society are sound. Meanwhile, the number of homeless people continues to increase, and good intentions and well-meaning volunteers have not been able to fill the void created by a lack of jobs that pay enough money to support a family.

Obviously, a business-as-usual approach is adequate as long as the pathways into homelessness represent individual failings. But homelessness in the last decade is representative of a growing economic dislocation, resulting from the failure of the U.S. economic system to adjust to world competitiveness. Most homeless people are not at fault for their plights. Instead, they are victims of an economic system that is increasingly mean-spirited.

The remainder of this chapter explores changes in the economic system that have placed greater numbers of individuals and families at risk for becoming homeless.

The Economics of Dislocation

Massive economic dislocation, resulting in homelessness, is not new to the American experience. The depression of 1870 and the Great Depression of 1933 were two such events (Piven & Cloward 1971). Society, however, has come to view such conditions as resulting from some climatic event that justifies the need for government intervention (Foner 1947).

In contrast to these "climatic events," the 1980s would appear to be times of unbounded prosperity. As a result, government intervention in the marketplace is frequently viewed as unnecessary and meddlesome. However, there are some parallels between the 1980s and the Great Depression of the 1930s. During the late 1920s, the stock market reached record highs. This boom was justified as resulting from the prosperity of the Coolidge and Hoover administrations, which was, in part, thought to have resulted from supply-side tax reductions (Galbraith 1987). The increasing supply of money helped to fuel speculation on the part of wealthy people. Paper profits mounted and investors were drawn into the market from a broader spectrum of economic groups. This process both increased the amount of capital available to business to engage in increased speculation (leveraged buy-outs through questionable security transactions), and broadened the risk to those, the middle class, who could least afford to lose their investments.

Holding companies began to proliferate and spin-off additional holding companies, which in turn engaged in leveraged buy-outs. New companies were formed as they merged with other companies, and the capital needed to float these purchases was created through the sell of preferred stock and junk bonds.

The concept of junk bonds is not new to the 1980s. During the 1920s, many highly leveraged corporations sold bonds that were rated very low because the combined assets, liabilities, and projected income of these corporations was not projected to be able to safely repay the bonds. As a result, the purchasers of these bonds were paid interest in excess of the market rate; however, since it was doubtful that the corporation in its present form could repay the bonds, they were rated as "junk."

The pyramiding of questionable corporate paper, such as junk bonds, depended in large part on the ability of corporations to make increasing profits. Otherwise, the ability of corporations to service their rapidly increasing debt was in jeopardy. At first glance, it appears that the run-up on Wall Street during the 1920s resulted from increased earnings. However, closer examination reveals that many corporations were buying other companies, selling off the more profitable portion of the acquired assets, and then using the revenues to repay debt and repurchase their own stock. Therefore, the rising profits were not based on business expanding to meet consumer demand. As a result, when demand fell or did not increase, the resulting fall in corporate earnings quickly created grave financial problems for both over-extended corporations and their creditors. In essence, the pyramid of highly leveraged and unsupported debt collapsed, and the shock waves resulted in massive unemployment and homelessness.

The picture of homelessness in the 1930s was seen as reflecting a heterogeneous group of individuals; some were looking for work, some found themselves on skid row because they had no pensions, and some were prevented from working by physical disabilities (Sutherland & Locke 1936). In the final analysis, however, these individuals were rejected because corporations no longer needed their services. It is true that researchers in the 1930s noted that some of the homeless (estimates vary from 14.5 to 30 percent), were frequent abusers of alcohol (Hoffer 1964). Nevertheless, the major reason for their homelessness was viewed by a large portion of society as resulting from the massive unemployment across the nation, and alcohol abuse was a consequence of their hopelessness. This distinction is important because the government largely defined the problem of homelessness as resulting from economic dislocation and suggested a wide variety of interventions designed to revive the economy.

During the 1980s, there has also been a highly speculative fervor in which corporate mergers, leveraged buy-outs, and questionable financial instruments, such as junk bonds, have become commonplace (Burck 1981; Cohran 1984). This activity reflects a drive for quick profits that manifests itself in the purchase of corporations and the selling off of the acquired company's more lucrative assets to pay the increasing dividends and interest needed to finance more takeovers.

Eastern Airlines provides an unfortunate example of this phenomenon. Texas Air purchased Eastern and immediately began raiding some of Eastern's cash flow and selling off some of its more profitable assets, such as Eastern's ticketing system, for less than fair market value. Texas Air, the parent holding company, profited. On the other hand, Eastern, in order to offset the cash raided by Texas Air, was confronted with a need to extract more surplus value from its workers. *Surplus value* is the difference between the value of work done or products produced and the wages paid by the employer. In the case of Eastern Airlines, Texas Air determined that wages had to be lowered in order to increase the surplus value. A fact overlooked by Texas Air, but not by the Machinist's Union of Eastern Airlines, is that by selling off assets, Texas Air had effectively lowered the productivity and surplus value of Eastern employees. Not wanting to have their wages reduced, Eastern employees struck the airlines and as a result they became vulnerable to homelessness.

The money to fuel the speculation, made possible through the purchase of and development of holding companies such as Texas Air, has been created by the supply-side tax policies of the Reagan administration. Much of Reagan's economic policies were based on the ideas of a young conservative economist named Arthur Laffer. His view was simple. Increased taxes would actually result in reduced revenue to the federal government because at some point (no one is sure where or when) taxes become so high that people loose their incentive to produce more income. As noted by Alperovitz and Faux (1984):

> It is like saying that there is a point at which another glass of milk will make you sick—undoubtedly true, but irrelevant unless you have already had as much milk as you can drink without being sick. The question was, were we at the place on the Laffer Curve at which people were already being taxed too much? Unfortunately, you could not tell from the Laffer Curve. It was freehand drawing, not a statistical chart. (p. 41)

In addition to the questionable soundness of the Laffer Curve is the fact that the majority of workers do not have the option of adjusting their earnings; instead, they work the same number of hours per week regardless of the tax rate. Therefore, the Laffer Curve is only applicable to the very wealthy.

A not so surprising result of the Reagan era tax cuts has been that the top 1 percent of households have been able to amass 34.3 percent of the wealth, a concentration paralleled only by the 1929 rate of 36.6 percent (Butra 1988). However, the wealthy have spent much of their new-found wealth on luxury items, such as expensive vacations, homes, and automobiles. Investment in corporate America as demonstrated by the decade-long run-up in stock prices has been created by a climate of speculative fervor in which corporations have purchased other corporations. In addition, many corporations have repurchased their outstanding stock. This process has artificially inflated prices and made it appear as if Wall Street was raising its evaluation of a particular corporation.

In addition, those wealthy individuals who have invested in the stock market have demanded higher rates of return. The fact that junk bonds were sold so easily is not surprising. Many middle-class individuals, not wanting to miss Wall Street's "roaring 80s," invested in the stock market. This in turn, much like the 1930s, increased the amount of capital available for overall speculation and increased the asset vulnerability of middle-class investors.

Pension fund managers also entered the market with increasing voracity, and quickly poured much of the fund's assets into buy-out schemes.

Unlike the 1920s, the U.S. economy of today has structural stabilizers, such as limits on stock margin accounts and federal insurance for deposits in commercial banks, to prevent a major depression. Whereas these stabilizers have averted a depression and kept corporations from becoming bankrupt, they have not, as in the Great Depression, cancelled the debts of major corporations. Consequently, today's corporations are having to service the debts they have incurred. This has resulted in serious setbacks in which thousands of employees have lost their jobs. Illustrative of what happens when a company engages in downsizing to either ward off a corporate takeover or create cash to service its highly leveraged position is the example of Time, Inc. One of the quickest ways a company can reduce its costs and conserve cash is to lay off workers or close down a portion of its operations. In 1981, Time, Inc., closed the 100-year-old *Washington Star* in Washington, D.C. As a result, hundreds of employees lost their jobs. In this game of high corporate stakes, the losers are the employees, who are simply a cost to be eliminated, and the community, which must bear the cost of supporting the victims of the lay-off. Meanwhile, the corporate entity is free to enter into more deals in which workers are displaced and communities are burdened with the costs of economic dislocation.

While some workers find other employment, others do not recover and are unable to find jobs in which they can support their families. The General Accounting Office estimated that from 1983 to 1984, a time of supposed economic recovery, 7,800 firms with 100 or more workers either shut down or laid off workers (Gainer 1986).

Today's relatively low unemployment rate of 4 to 5 percent would seem to compare favorably with the fact that in 1933, one-third or 33 percent of the work force was out of work (Nathan 1936). While many policy makers argue that only 4 to 5 percent of the work force is currently unemployed, it should be noted that society has no way of knowing how many people are underemployed or how many have quit looking for work. In fact, some social scientists suspect that the government underestimates the extent of unemployment by 50 to 300 percent (Kogut & Aron 1980; Yankelovich et al. 1983). In addition, the proliferation of low-wage work [as noted by Bluestone and Harrison (1982) and Harrison and Bluestone (1988)] and the increase of the working poor support the suspicion that the 4 or 5 percent official unemployment rate does not accurately reflect the economic health of this country. More important, a low unemployment rate allows policy makers to blame homeless people for their plight and to ignore economic dislocation as a factor in causing homelessness.

Official unemployment statistics also fail to account for the prevailing wage rates of those employed. For example, many economists have warned that the low unemployment rate will lead to wage inflation as companies have to pay higher wages to attract workers. It is true that companies are having difficulty attracting entry-level workers (Reamer 1988). However, this reflects the fact that "entry-level workers," which is the new euphemism for the lowest paid unskilled workers, are not able to find an adequate supply of low-income housing. It is not a question of too many people being employed. Instead, the high wage rates being paid to entry-level workers reflect the high cost of housing. Not surprisingly, wage pressure is greatest where the housing problems are the worst (Putka 1989). For example, Montgomery County, Maryland, an area with extremely high housing costs, is having to bus in entry-level workers from the neighboring District of Columbia, which has a supply of cheap labor. This example emphasizes that some parts of the country may be overheated, in that firms, such as fast-food restaurants, have to pay higher wages to attract entry-level workers. However, the country as a whole is not experiencing a high rate of inflation associated with a fully employed labor force.

Business success in the 1980s and 1990s is defined by short-term profits created by minimal investment and short-term cost reductions. This managerial style has played a major role in undermining the vigor of American industry (Hayes & Abernathy 1980). The effects on workers of these policies is reflected in the growing number of unemployed and underemployed and in the rise in poverty.

Unemployment, Underemployment, and the Poor

Perhaps the reason that economic indicators, such as the unemployment rate, are misleading is that management would prefer not to be judged by its effectiveness in extracting more surplus value from its workers. This refers to the notion that workers produce a product that is worth more than they are paid. As a result, workers produce a surplus value. In a capitalist economy management's apparent goal is to keep the amount of surplus value returned to a worker at a bare minimum.

In addition, it is in the government's best interest to maintain the appearance of low unemployment rates. Otherwise, groups could potentially leverage more money for the poor and unemployed. As a result, the economic indicators tend to confuse and obscure the effects of economic changes on the economy and, more important, on workers. For example, corporations in the last two decades have found it increasingly difficult to exploit cheap labor within the boundaries of developed nations (Palloix 1977; Slater 1985). As a result, corporate profits during the 1970s and early 1980s were in jeopardy. This in turn has resulted in the substitution of capital for labor in which firms invested in goods and services that could be created more cheaply and result in higher profit margins. For example, financial services, which are a service-sector industry, have grown dramatically over the past decade. In addition, the work force within this industry has been reduced by using computers (Fabricant 1987). Consequently, workers are increasingly being employed in the lower-paid service-sector economy, where greater output is expected for less pay. Finally, firms are attempting to reduce the total number of workers by automating as many jobs as possible.

While this substitution may enable management to obtain higher profits, the effect on labor is obvious. Some jobs will be eliminated, such as in heavy manufacturing. Those remaining, such as in fast-food restaurants, will pay lower wages as a result of the lower surplus value that can be extracted from workers.

The second way capital is substituted for labor is through mergers and acquisitions in which corporations purchase other firms and then quickly sell the most profitable assets of the companies acquired. Business leaders argue that corporations have become healthier as a result because buying capabilities have been expanded and unhealthy capital investments have been purged (Burck 1981). However, what is considered an unhealthy investment must be closely examined. The current business climate judges long-term investments, such as an investment in upgrading plant and equipment, as unhealthy because the short-term return will be negligible. On the other hand, an investment in which another business is purchased and its assets sold will yield short-term profits and, therefore, is considered a solid investment. These mergers, however, while increasing the income statement for a corporation, will immediately reduce jobs. Over the long-term, the effect of these transactions will result in a lower-paid work force.

Since many corporations have not made sufficient investments in research and development or in upgrading their plant and equipment, they will be unable to make a better mousetrap. In effect, because they have squandered their investment capital through corporate mergers instead of investing in new technology, they will have to reduce the wages they pay workers. Such practices have been referred to as creating a "hollow corporation" in which firms generally lack the resources to maintain themselves (Jonas 1986).

Ultimately, fewer jobs and a decline in the types of jobs that require minimal skills but pay relatively high wages creates a situation in which some individuals are not able to purchase many of the products and services, including housing, created by the economy. However, the fact that the economy has not slid into a depression leads people to think that the high rates of poverty and homelessness are not associated with the actions of corporate America. In fact, critics question the notion that a weak economy is to blame for the rise in the homeless population, when unemployment is historically low and the majority of Americans appear to be prospering.

The notion that the economy is doing well, since the nation is not in a depression, depends on what social class is being examined. Certainly, the upper middle class is enjoying economic prosperity. However, the urban poor are increasingly having to live in isolated, damaging, and "mean-spirited" environments (Burgdoff & Bell 1984). The urban underclass is certainly one of the groups that has been adversely affected by the decline in manufacturing jobs (Gephart & Pearson 1988).

The percentage of poor people living in central cities has dramatically increased from a low of 27 percent in 1959 to over 43 percent by 1985 (U.S. Bureau of the Census 1982, 1985). Chicago's North Lawndale, a black community on the city's West Side, provides a vivid example of the concentration of poverty characteristic of many central cities. Since 1960, over half the housing stock has disappeared, and the remainder is in bad repair. The murder rate in 1985 was six times that of the nation overall. Unwed teenage pregnancies accounted for 70 percent of all babies born in the community.

One of the reasons for these conditions is the high unemployment rate. Today, North Lawndale has lost 75 percent of its business establishments, over 67,000 jobs, and those businesses left are state lottery agents, currency agents, and liquor stores (Wacquant & Wilson 1988). Central cities across the nation are experiencing similar problems. Kasarda (1988) observes:

> Between 1953 and 1985, for example, New York City lost over 600,000 jobs in manufacturing, while white-collar service jobs grew by nearly 800,000. During this period, Philadelphia lost more than two-thirds of its manufacturing jobs. Manufacturing employment in Boston declined from 114,000 to 49,000; in Baltimore, from 130,000 to 55,000; and in St. Louis, from 194,000 to 66,000. (p. 171)

No one knows for certain how many residents in these communities are homeless; however, with virtually no jobs, homelessness is inevitable.

In urban areas, underemployment is "more likely to take the form of full-time, year-round, low-wage work . . ." (Harrison & Bluestone 1988, p. 72). Those just above the poverty line also are vulnerable to homelessness. These individuals are frequently referred to as "income marginals" (Rodgers 1982) because they experience frequent unemployment and they must struggle to pay their mortgage payments or rent and keep their aging cars on the road (Wyers 1988). In 1983, at least 11 million Americans were determined to be just above the poverty level (Wyers 1988). Poverty and homelessness are just around the corner for these people, and any mistake or bad luck can cause great economic hardship.

The fact that many Americans, particularly the poor and the near poor, confront increasing difficulty in obtaining affordable housing can be explained in part by the dramatic decline in manufacturing. This decrease, however, has been accompanied by a dramatic growth in service-sector jobs. Instead of recovery, the new jobs of the 1990s raise the prospect that the living conditions of the poor and near poor will become more desperate.

The New Jobs of the 1990s and Homelessness

Over the last fifteen years, the American economy has undergone a dramatic shift in which management has worked hard to reduce the wages they pay workers and in the process exploit a greater surplus value. In the majority of cases this has occurred by switching from manufacturing to services. Gone forever are many manufacturing jobs that once employed unskilled and low-educated individuals at wages with which they could afford to support themselves. Between January 1981 and January 1986, a total of 10.8 million workers lost their jobs because of plant closings or employment cutbacks (Horvath 1987). By 1986, just 67 percent of these individuals had found jobs. Those who had lost managerial or professional jobs (service) were 75 percent more likely to find new jobs. On the other hand, those who were employed as operators, fabricators, and laborers (manufacturing) were reemployed in only 66 percent of the cases (Horvath 1987). Those individuals who found work in the services industry often earned as much as 40 percent less than those in manufacturing.

As the number of manufacturing jobs decreased, service jobs began to account for a greater percentage of employed individuals. Not surprisingly, wages and salaries peaked in the early to mid-1970s, and they are now at approximately the same level in constant dollars as in 1960 (Annual Report of the Council of Economic Advisers 1987). Meanwhile, prices have more than tripled and continue to rise.

The traditionally low wages paid by service-sector employers is made worse by the fact that service employees typically receive only 25 percent of employer contributions to private welfare funds, such as pensions, health care insurance, and educational benefits (National Income and Products Account 1986). Another sign of lower income groups and even some in the middle class being worse off is illustrated by the personal savings rate. Between 1970 and 1980, personal savings amounted to 7.9 percent of disposable personal income. The rate then declined from 6.1 to 3.8 percent between 1984 and 1988 (Annual Report of the Council of Economic Advisers 1988). The low personal savings rate reflects the fact that family incomes have declined among all groups, except those earning $50,000 or more a year (Horrigan & Haugen 1988). Even this statistic is misleading, because many of the families with earnings above $50,000 are composed of two wage earners, the husband and wife, as opposed to previous decades when one wage earner was able to earn enough to be included in the middle class. The decline of the middle class is therefore debated, and many conservative economists overlook the composition of today's dual-income family.

The decline in manufacturing jobs began in the 1970s when U.S. corporations were confronted for the first time with significant overseas competition (Thurow 1984). Rather than develop new technologies, invest in aging plants and equipment, or retrain their work force, U.S. companies made the decision to restructure their assets toward a service-dominated economy. Harrison (1987) observes: "The captains of American industry could not figure out how to produce fresh products, improve the quality of old ones, or even market the ones they had" (p. 7). At the same time, supply-side tax cuts increased the pool of available capital needed for corporate restructuring. Also noteworthy is the use of the federal tax system to reduce the cost of plant closures for corporations. For example, Harrison and Bluestone (1988) note that corporations such as United Technologies and Crown Zellerbach "earned" a total of $672 million dollars by closing facilities.

The U.S. government made it possible for large corporations to switch to service employment by subsidizing the cost of the changeover. Service-sector jobs can be classified into two groups: professionals and technicians who are reasonably well-paid; and salesclerks, clerical workers, maids, and restaurant workers who receive relatively low pay and few benefits. It is estimated that 50 percent of private employees work in the second category of service-sector jobs.

The growth of the service sector is illustrated by the State of Maryland, where between 1980 and 1986 the service industry became a leader among all Maryland industries. Service-sector jobs represented 64.3 percent of the new jobs created, whereas manufacturing jobs, particularly in the durable goods sector, declined by 11.4 percent (Maryland Department of Economic and Employment Development 1987). By the year 2000, service occupations nationwide are projected to increase 25 percent, whereas manufacturing is projected to decline by 2 percent (Silvestri and Lukasiewicz 1987). It should be noted, however, that manufacturing already accounts for only 14.6 of the work force.

The decline in manufacturing jobs has been most significant for black youths who drop out of high school. In 1974, for example, 91 percent of this group was employed, mostly in manufacturing jobs. By 1986, the number of unemployed black youths without a high school degree had risen to 15.7 percent (Ballen & Freeman 1986). Once again, we must point out that this number is an underestimate because it does not reflect those individuals who simply stopped looking for work.

The exporting of jobs overseas has contributed to the decline in manufacturing jobs and the transition to service-sector jobs. U.S. corporations have been adept at developing world market factories in less-developed countries. Locating overseas has saved American corporations millions of dollars because they encounter fewer government controls, less-stringent pollution standards, lower wage rates, few fringe benefits, and a more desperate and compliant work force (Seamonds 1985). In 1981, overseas tax shelters enabled large corporations with profits between $1.1 billion and $9.6 billion to receive tax refunds or to owe no taxes (Bell 1987).

Businesses have blamed the American worker for this flight overseas. For example, the steel industry has continually criticized workers for demanding high wages. However, this enables steel corporations to *not* take responsibility for their bad investments, failure to upgrade equipment, and diversification into areas outside their business expertise. Coupled with the continuing decline of manufacturing jobs, U.S. corporations have been able to engage in a practice referred to as "whipsawing" in which they bully their workers into accepting wage reductions (Harrison 1987). Another popular effort used to reduce wages and overhead is through the downsizing of full-time jobs into part-time jobs. Projections on the new jobs created through the year 2000 show that a great proportion will be part-time, for which workers will be employed at low wages (Uchitelle 1987). A study in 1984 found that part-time employees were paid lower hourly wages and received little, if any, health insurance coverage (Ehrenberg et al. 1988).

The proliferation of low-wage work is illustrated by the fact that between 1979 and 1985 only 6 percent of the new jobs in manufacturing paid wages below $7,400 per year, whereas in the service sector the number is 40 percent (Harrison 1987). This increase comes at a time when median gross rent is rising at a rate equal to 29 percent of median income. As a result, more than 6.3 million Americans pay more than 50 percent of their income for rent (Hartman 1987). By the year 2003, it is estimated that 18.7 million Americans will be unable to afford housing (Dreier 1988).

The fact that wages in the rapidly increasing service sector are pegged to the minimum wage is overlooked by most policy makers. Instead, there is a tendency to pretend that the minimum wage only affects teenagers and entry-level workers. In fact, in 1986, annual wages in retailing averaged $9,036, or $2,000 less than the poverty level for a family of four (Moorehouse & Dembo 1986). Also noteworthy is that wages in retailing average only 44.3 percent of wages in manufacturing. This means that wages in manufacturing averaged approximately $20,500, or $10 an hour in 1986, whereas wages in retailing averaged approximately $9,036, or $4.42 an hour.

In effect, many American workers and their families are being pushed into poverty by the shift to a service-dominated economy. The fact that homelessness has dramatically risen over the last decade is not simply a coincidence. Instead, it is related to economic dislocation resulting from changing employment patterns.

The U.S. Conference of Mayors (1987) has made painfully clear the effects of the unavailability of manufacturing jobs, the increase in low-paying service-sector jobs, and the increase in the cost of housing. The central cities are described as "nightmares waiting to happen." The riots in the fall of 1988 in Miami were the result of desperate people with little or no hope for the future. Like most urban riots, the police made an arrest, which sparked the pent-up frustrations, anger, and hopelessness of urban ghetto residents. The residents of central cities want attention in the form of jobs, decent housing, and city services. Instead, their governments give them extra police patrols and call for more prison beds.

Homelessness is no longer an accident; instead, it is simply a result of chronic unemployment, underemployment, and a scarcity of low- to moderate-income housing. Not surprisingly, homelessness has increased 17 percent between 1986 and 1987 (U.S. Conference of Mayors 1987).

Critics have charged that our portrayal of homelessness overlooks the fact that many among the homeless are mothers on Aid to Families with Dependent Children (AFDC) or people, such as the elderly, who are dependent on society. In other words, our critics claim that a change in the employment patterns of American workers should have little effect on these individuals, since they are not in the job market. While it is true these individuals are not generally in the job market, the value of welfare benefits has fallen, despite an increase in the amount of the total federal expenditure on AFDC (Danziger & Plotnick 1986). Expenditure increases have not kept pace with inflation, while the number of recipients has continued to rise. Therefore, some homelessness is going to occur among AFDC recipients because their payments do not keep pace with the cost of housing. Between 1980 and 1984, the number of AFDC and child welfare programs declined by 13 percent (Horowitz & Lay 1984). In addition, 90 percent of the working families on AFDC had their benefits reduced or eliminated (Brodkin & Lipsky 1983).

This analysis, however, is also incomplete, because the total number of families seeking substandard and low-rental housing is increasing at the same time as the supply of such housing is decreasing. In addition to families on AFDC seeking low-income housing, there are now individuals who have been priced out of more expensive housing markets because of the decline in their wages and the increase in housing prices. This competition for low-income housing has taken place during the Reagan era, when there has been a 75 percent cutback in funds for low-income housing (Dreier 1987). The overall effect of this low-income housing shortage has been to make the price of existing low-income housing rise. Therefore, the competition for truly low-income housing is stiff, and many AFDC families lose out in the competition to marginally employed workers. If U.S. policy would change to encourage the growth of the manufacturing sector, these marginally employed workers would increase their standards of living and leave low-income housing to families on AFDC. Therefore, the increasing number of AFDC families among the homeless is directly related to the decline in manufacturing jobs, the increase in low-wage service-sector jobs, and an overall increase in the number of families who can only afford to live in low-income and substandard housing.

Looking Ahead

The notion that much of the homelessness in the 1980s is a direct result of economic dislocation is difficult to empirically establish. As already noted, the homeless represent, in many ways, an invisible underclass. They often do not appear on unemployment rolls and are therefore not included in *official* unemployment statistics. In addition, census data is noted for its under-counting of people in urban areas (Porter 1989).

As we have already noted, the homeless live with family and friends, in abandoned buildings, under bridges, on the streets, in jails and hospitals, and in shelters. Denied access to mainstream America, many homeless people have created their own world, filled with desperation and quiet suffering. Under-standing their plight is possible, but it requires abandoning biases that portray them all as representing a group of pathological misfits.

It is not that many Americans are unable to put aside their prejudices of homeless people. Perhaps, we, as a society, are uncertain of our future and, more important, of our own ability to prosper. As a result, the homeless are viewed with both disdain and curiosity. They are seen with disdain because they raise doubts about the ability of our economic system to create pros-perity. On the other hand, society is curious about their plight because they are, in the end, human beings, like us.

Thus far, however, the disdain and curiosity have not combined to create a demand for more information about specific pathways that create homeless-ness. Society appears to be content to develop more and improved shelters. The problem continues to grow, however, and shelters seem to offer nothing in the way of a solution.

Perhaps the prevailing framework used to understand social problems is biased in favor of absolving the prevailing economic system of responsibility. Future analyses of social problems need to abandon conventional wisdom that absolves the current economic system from causing homelessness. We have sought to critically examine the economic events over the last decade and sug-gest that a model of economic dislocation is responsible for much of the sharp increase in homelessness.

The United States has never been particularly good at admitting when its citizens are in need of government assistance. In addition, we, as a society, have not been particularly adept at designing and implementing reforms of this nature. Even the reforms after the Great Depression of the 1930s were designed to avoid widespread unrest and enable the economy to mature with-out self-destruction (Kolko 1963; Weinstein 1968). There is little doubt that these reforms served the interests of business; nevertheless, for a short time, from 1940–1970, homelessness was prevented from reaching crisis propor-tions.

The New Deal and its hodgepodge of programs, such as the Works Pro-gress Administration (WPA), did not end the depression. It took World War II with its full employment to bring about economic prosperity. In many ways, despite his apparent liberalism, Roosevelt wanted to make sure that the New Deal did not take away the work incentive among the nation's unemployed. Therefore, much like its successor, the Great Society of the 1960s, the New Deal did more to keep the populace from rioting and destroying capitalism than it did to actually stimulate the economy. Actual reforms, such as those to limit the amount of margin one could use to purchase stocks, were designed to keep the structures of the economy, such as Wall Street, from self-destructing.

Since then, capitalism has matured, and new reforms are needed to prevent economic dislocation. Otherwise, businesses will find it increasingly difficult to compete in world markets, and more individuals will become vulnerable to poverty and eventual homelessness. It would be naive to suggest that changes in the economy will prevent all people from falling into poverty and eventual homelessness. There will always be those individuals who, largely as a result of their own incompatibilities and mistakes, fail to take advantage of opportunities, squander their earnings, and become homeless.

On the other hand, it is difficult to neatly separate those who are homeless because of economic dislocation and those who are homeless because of individual failings. The unemployed individual who did not save enough money to pay rent because he or she needed the money to satisfy an alcohol abuse problem, and is subsequently evicted, is certainly imprudent. If, however, this individual believed he or she would not find a job because of long-term unemployment, then alcohol abuse is a reaction to negative circumstances. Perhaps, if the person lived in a society with full employment, he or she would be less likely to abuse alcohol.

The notion that the poor are in one way or another victims of an unjust social system has been labeled by conservatives and neo-liberals alike as "too permissive." Some conservative essayists, such as Tyrell (1984), deride notions that suggest corporate America could ever do anything that is not in the public good. Smoke and mirrors, through efforts such as voluntarism, have come to symbolize this nation's commitment to the poor. In keeping with this tradition, George Bush has promised a "kinder, gentler nation." The substance of his programs thus far, however, has favored the wealthy with approaches such as a significant decrease in the capital gains tax. At the same time, those who fall victim to the increasing economic insecurity of a service-dominated economy are blamed for their failings.

Basically, we, as a society, are at a crossroads in regards to resolving the problem of homelessness. On one hand, more legislation such as the McKinney Act, which increased the amount of money available for shelters but did not in any way address the changes in employment patterns, can be developed. On the other hand, society could choose to resolve the crisis of homelessness by creating more stability in the marketplace.

Essentially, our economic dislocation model raises for critical analysis values of fairness, equity, and justice. Rather than assume values are not appropriate subjects for debate and policy analysis, we believe it is important to critically analyze the values that support public policies. Rein (1978) observes, "a value-critical position treats values not merely as the accepted aims of policy but as a subject for debate and analysis" (p. 73). Whereas those in power may argue that some economic dislocation is necessary in order for the economy to prosper, it is interesting to note that they are not the ones who suffer—they generally prosper as a result of the chaos caused by economic dislocation. For example, the recession of 1980–82, which was created by the policies of the Reagan administration, resulted in increased unemployment and poverty. The ones who were the most likely to be forced into poverty, however, were those who were already at the margins or who were part of the lower middle class. More wealthy individuals, on the other hand, witnessed an increase in their stock portfolios as companies were able to reduce expenses.

Therefore, homelessness is not without its benefits—it depends upon your vantage point. From the vantage point of a company threatening to lock out workers rather than meet their wage demands, the threat of homelessness can be used as a sobering reminder of the effects of having no income or a much smaller income.

It is this fact that the economic dislocation model highlights. Rather than portray homelessness as a state of affairs that occurs by accident, we argue that much of it is a logical result of policies designed to change employment and investment patterns. Admittedly, new policies to address the crisis of homelessness will require hard choices. But in the end, wealth will have to be redistributed through a more progressive tax structure that creates an economy capable of employing more Americans so they can participate in the mainstream economy. Before exploring specific approaches, however, the next chapter will examine an exploratory study of homelessness that led to the development of the economic dislocation hypothesis.

References

Alperovitz, G. & Faux, J. (1984). *Rebuilding America*. New York: Pantheon Books.

Anderson, M. (1978). *Welfare: The Political Economy of Welfare Reform in the United States*. Stanford, CA: Hoover Institution.

Annual Report of the Council of Economic Advisers (1987). Washington, D.C.: Government Printing Office, Tables B–24, B–26.

——— (1988). Washington, D.C.: Government Printing Office, Tables B–24, B–26.

Arce, A.A., Tadlock, M., Vergare, M.J. & Shapiro, S.H. (1983). A psychiatric profile of street people admitted to emergency shelter. *Hospital and Community Psychiatry, 34,* 812.

Ballen, J. & Freeman, R.B. (1986). Transition between employment and nonemployment. In Freeman, R.B. & Holzer, H.J. (eds.), *The Black Youth Employment Crisis*. Chicago: National Bureau of Economic Research.

Belcher, J.R. (1988). Are jails replacing the mental health system for the homeless mentally ill? *Community Mental Health Journal, 24,* 3: 185–95.

Belcher, J.R. & Toomey, B.G. (1988). Relationship between the deinstitutionalization model, psychiatric disability, and homelessness. *Health and Social Work, 13,* (2): 145–53.

Bell, W. (1987). *Contemporary Social Welfare.* New York: Macmillan.

Bluestone, B. & Harrison, B. (1982). *The Deindustrialization of America.* New York: Basic Books, Inc.

Brodkin, E. & Lipsky, M. (1983). Quality control in A.F.D.C. as an administrative strategy. *Social Service Review,* March.

Burck, A. (1981). A different opinion: A merger specialist who hates mergers. *Fortune, 108,* 221–28.

Burgdoff, R. & Bell, C. (1984). *The Employment of the Full Spectrum Abilities.* Washington, D.C.: U.S. Civil Rights Commission.

Butra, R. (1988). *The Great Depression of 1990.* New York: Dell Books.

Cohran, B. (1984). *Welfare Capitalism—And After.* New York: Schocken Books.

Danziger, S.H. & Plotnick, R.D. (1986). Poverty and policy: Lessons from the last two decades. *Social Service Review, 60,* (1): 34–51.

Dreier, P. (1987). Community-based housing: A progressive approach to a new federal policy. *Social Policy, 17,* 18–22.

Ehrenberg, R., Rosenberg, P. & Li, J. (1988). Part time employment in the United States. In Hart, R. (ed.), *Employment and Hours of Work.* London: George Allen and Unwin.

Fabricant, M. (1987). The political economy of homelessness. *Catalyst, 21,* 11–28.

Farr, R.K. (1984). The Los Angeles Skid Row Mental Health Project. *Psychosocial Rehabilitation Journal, 8,* 2 Oct: 64–76.

Fischer, P.J., Shapiro, S., Breakey, W.R., Anthony, J.C. & Kramer, M. (1986). Mental health and social characteristics of the homeless: A survey of mission users. *American Journal of Public Health, 76,* 519–23.

Foner, P.S. (1947). *History of the Labor Movement in the United States.* New York: International Publishers.

Gainer, W.J. (1986). U.S. Business Closures and Permanent Layoffs during 1983 and 1984. OTA—GAO Workshop on Plant Closings, 20 April–1 May, 3.

Galbraith, J.K. (1987). The 1929 parallel. *The Atlantic Monthly,* January, 62–66.

Gephart, M.A. & Pearson, R.W. (1988). Contemporary research on the urban underclass. *ITEM, 42,* 1/2: 1–10.

Harrison, B. (1987). The impact of corporate restructuring on labor income. *Social Policy, 17,* 6–11.

Harrison, B. & Bluestone, B. (1988). *The Great U-Turn: Corporate Restructuring and the Polarizing of America.* New York: Basic Books, Inc.

Hartman, C. (1987). The Housing Part of the Homelessness Problem. In *Homelessness: Critical Issues for Policy and Practice.* Boston: The Boston Foundation.

Hayes, R. & Abernathy, W. (1980). Managing our way to economic decline. *Harvard Business Review,* July–August.

Hoffer, E. (1964). *The Ordeal of Change.* New York: Harper & Row.

Horowitz, M. & Lay, I. et al. (1984). *The State, the People, and the Reagan Cuts: An Analysis of Social Spending Cuts.* Washington, D.C.: AFSCME.

Horrigan, M.W. & Haugen, S.E. (1988). The Declining middle-class thesis: A sensitivity analysis. *Monthly Labor Review, 111,* (5): 3–13.

Horvarth, F.E. (1987). The pulse of economic change: Displaced workers of 1981–1985. *Monthly Labor Review, 110,* 3–12.

Jonas, N. (1986). The hollow corporation. *Business Week, March 3,* 58–9.

Karno, M., Brunam, R.L., Melonie, A., Escobar, J.I., Timbers, D.M., Santana, F. & Boyd, J.H. (1987). Life-time prevalence of specific psychiatric disorders among Mexican-Americans and non-Hispanic whites in Los Angeles. *Archives of General Psychiatry, 44,* (7): 695–709.

Kasarda, J.D. (1988). Jobs, migration, and emerging urban mismatches. In McGeary, M.G.H. & Lynn, L.E., Jr. (eds.), *Urban Change and Poverty.* Washington, D.C.: National Academy Press.

Kogut, A. & Aron, S. (1980). Toward a full employment policy: An overview. *Journal of Sociology and Social Welfare, 7,* 85–99.

Kolko, G. (1963). *The Triumph of Conservatism: A Reinterpretation of American History, 1900–1916.* New York: Free Press.

Maryland Department of Economic and Employment Development (1987). *Manufacturing Industry in Maryland: 1980–1986.* Baltimore, MDEED.

Milburn, N.G. & Watts, R.J. (1985–86). Methodological issues in research on the homeless and the homeless mentally ill. *International Journal of Mental Health, 14,* 4: 42–60.

Moorehouse, W. & Dembo, D. (1986). The underbelly of the U.S. economy: Joblessness and pauperization of working America. Special Report no. 6. New York: Council on International and Public Affairs.

Murray, C.A. (1984). *Losing Ground: American Social Policy, 1950–80.* New York: Basic Books, Inc.

Nathan, R.R. (1936). *Estimates of Unemployment in the United States, 1929–35.* Geneva: International Labour Office.

National Income and Products Account (1986). Tables 6.4b, 6.5b, 6.6b. Washington, D.C.: U.S. Department of Commerce.

Palloix, C. (1977). The self-explanation of capital on a world scale. *Review of Radical Political Economics, 9,* 2: 1–28.

Perr, I.N. (1985). The malignant neglect of the mentally ill street people. *American Journal of Psychiatry, 142,* 7: 885–86.

Piven, F.F. & Cloward, R.A. (1971). *Regulating the Poor: The Functions of Public Welfare.* New York: Vintage Books.

Porter, K.H. (1989). *Poverty in Rural America: A National Overview.* Washington, D.C.: Center on Budget and Policy Priorities.

Putka, G. (1989). Massachusetts suffers as its revenues lag and route 128 falters. *The Wall Street Journal,* Wednesday, February 9, 1.

Reamer, F.G. (1988). The affordable housing crisis and social work. *Social Work, 34,* 5–9.

Rein, M. (1978). *Social Science/Public Policy.* Kingsport, TN: Kingsport Press.

Rich, S. (1988). Urban Institute study puts number of U.S. homeless at close to 300,000. *Washington Post,* Friday, Nov. 4, A10.

Rodgers, H.R., Jr. (1982). *The Cost of Human Neglect.* Cambridge, MA: Harvard University Press.

Rooney, J. (1980). Organizational success through program failures: Skid row mission. *Social Forces, 58,* 904.

Seamonds, J.A. (1985). When states go all out to lure industry. *U.S. News & World Report, 98,* (May 20): 92.

Segal, S.P., Baumohl, J. & Johnson, E. (1977). Falling through the cracks: Mental disorder and social margin in a young vagrant population. *Social Problems, 24,* 387.

Silvestri, G.T. & Lukasiewicz, M. (1987). A look at occupational employment trends to the year 2000. *Monthly Labor Review, 110,* 9: 46–63.

Slater, D. (1985). *Territory and State in Latin America.* London: Macmillan.

Stockman, D. (1986). *The Triumph of Politics.* New York: Harper & Row.

Sutherland, E.H. & Locke, H.J. (1936). *Twenty Thousand Homeless Men: A Study of Unemployed Men in Chicago Shelters.* Chicago: J.B. Lippincott.

Thurow, L.C. (1984). A world class economy. *Tocqueville Review, 6,* 303–26.

Tyrell, R.E. (1984). *The Liberal Crack-up.* New York: Simon & Schuster.

Uchitelle, L. (1987). Making a living is now a family enterprise. *New York Times Careers Section,* 11, October, 6, 8.

U.S. Bureau of Census (1982). Characteristics of the population below poverty levels: 1980. *CPS Reports.* Washington, D.C.

———— (1985). Money income and poverty status of families and persons in the United States: 1985. *CPS Reports.* Washington, D.C.

U.S. Conference of Mayors (1987). *A Status Report on Homeless Families in America's Cities.* Washington, D.C.: The U.S. Conference of Mayors, May.

Wacquant, L.J.D. & Wilson, W.J. (1988). Beyond welfare reform: Poverty, joblessness, and social transformation of the inner city. Paper presented at the Rockefeller Foundation Conference on Welfare Reform. Williamsburg, VA.

Wallace, S. (1968). The road to skid row. *Social Problems, 16,* 92.

Weinstein, J. (1968). *The Corporate Ideal in the Liberal State: 1900–1918.* Boston: Beacon Press.

Wilson, W.J. (1987). *The Truly Disadvantaged.* Chicago: University of Chicago Press.

Wyers, N.L. (1988). Economic insecurity: Notes for Social Workers. *Social Work, 33,* 1: 18–22.

Yankelovich, D., et al. (1983). *Work and Human Values: An International Report on Jobs in the 1980s and 1990s.* New York: Aspen Institute.

2
Understanding Dislocation Theory Through Exploratory Research

D espite the interest in the plight of the homeless as a major social problem of the 1980s and 1990s, research understanding is largely undeveloped. Studies of homelessness have focused on prevalence and incidence and demographical categories. Although descriptive examinations contribute valuable information, they have not addressed causal factors, such as economic dislocation. This results in a deficiency in knowledge-building because the study of homelessness has been only loosely linked to theoretical explanations.

Not only has there been a lack of theoretical structure, but also the research has few bivariate and multivariate analyses. Data that are generated from homeless samples are often from univariate designs. Although these studies contribute information about the problem, they offer little knowledge of associations found through bivariate approaches and none of the controls in multivariate designs.

Economic dislocation of homeless people involves complex interactive factors that require sophisticated research methodologies. The combined evidence from descriptive studies suggests that homelessness is not a unitary phenomenon; therefore, to assess the relative and cumulative effects of relevant factors, bivariate and multivariate statistical procedures must be employed.

Despite the hypothesized potential of economic dislocation to explain homelessness, it has received no attention as a primary consideration in scientific studies to date. Hence, we are only at the frontier of the issue and must proceed in an exploratory fashion.

This chapter presents the research that lead us to develop the hypothesis that economic dislocation is one major cause of homelessness. In a joint effort with the Maryland Department of Human Resources, we set out to understand the incidence and nature of homelessness in Maryland and to get first-hand knowledge of the needs and services that homeless people were requesting. Surprisingly, we discovered that over one-third of the homeless were employed and that certain demographic variables were predictive of employment (DiBlasio et al. unpublished manuscript). Here we analyze the data from the rigor of a multivariate design and compare our results with the previous bivariate results. From the findings of this exploratory study, we formulate implications for research that might actually test the hypothesis of economic dislocation.

Methodology

Subjects and Sampling Procedure

Homeless people (n = 178) who entered one of the twenty-five Maryland shelters selected for the study were interviewed on a spring night by two research assistants. A questionnaire was administered to subjects in a confidential area of the shelter. The questionnaire contained structured categories for responses on a wide variety of information. Participation in the study was voluntary, and subjects were assured of confidentiality and the anonymity of their responses. The sites were stratified to represent the state's planning regions and to balance clientele, that is, shelters serving men, women, or families. The sample was 55 percent male (n = 98) and 45 percent female (n = 80). The ethnic composition was 48 percent white (n = 86), 48 percent black (n = 85), and 4 percent other (n = 7). Subjects ranged in age from 16 to 78. Interestingly, 54 percent (n = 94) of the total sample were parents.

Dependent and Independent Variables

From a conceptual standpoint, the dependent variable is best understood in two categories: the first representing those with no employment and the second representing those who are *underemployed* (defined as full- or part-time employment that does not provide sufficient income to pay for survival needs). This form of the variable is used in the logistical regression. However, in the zero-ordered correlations reported below, we analyzed the dependent variable in its original form (1 = unemployed; 2 = part-time; 3 = full-time) to provide an ordinal level approach for comparisons with the bivariate analysis in the earlier study (DiBlasio, et al. unpublished manuscript; henceforth "earlier study").

The following were among the demographic and other variables used as independent variables: gender; marital status (married/not currently married); ethnicity (non-white, white); military status (no military experience/some experience); and disability (disabled/not disabled). Several variables were coded on three-point to five-point scales for the frequency distributions and bivariate analysis (Pearson's) and later collapsed for the logistical analysis: (a) education (1 = 8th grade or less, 2 = 9th to 11th grade, 3 = high school degree, 4 = some college and above), collapsed form: (1 = no high school degree, 2 = high school degree or above); (b) health (1 = five or more health complaints, 2 = one to four health complaints, 3 = no health complaints); collapsed form: (1 = two or more health complaints, 2 = one or less health complaints) (a limitation of this variable is that it did not measure or weigh level of intensity of each health complaint); (c) food deprivation (1 = none, 2 = one to five days without eating, 3 = six or more days without eating); collapsed form: (1 = none, 2 = one or more days); (d) alcohol use (1 = a lot, 2 = some, 3 = none); collapsed form: (1 = use a lot of the time, 2 = use some or none of the time); (e) age (1 = 16 to 24 years, 2 = 25 to 34 years, 3 = 35 to 44 years, 4 = 45 to 54 years, 5 = 55 to 78 years).

Subjects were also asked to indicate whether or not they needed the following services (coded 0 = no; 1 = yes): job training; assistance locating housing; assistance in finding employment; social service benefits; casework advocacy; medical services; budget counseling; child care; parent skill training; transportation; drug/alcohol treatment; social skill training; counseling services; and educational services.

Results

Bivariate Findings

Of particular interest to the theory of economic dislocation is the finding that 35 percent (n = 62) of the subjects were employed in either full-time or part-time positions: 24 percent full-time and 11 percent part-time (see table 2–1). Whereas 70 percent of full-time employees were in permanent full-time positions, only 21 percent of the part-time workers were in permanent positions. Many of the temporary part-time positions included workfare, day labor, and migrant seasonal work.

Non-employed subjects reported the following reasons that their last job ended: 25 percent (n = 26) quit; 11 percent (n = 12) company closed/moved or laid-off; 11 percent (n = 12) poor health; 9 percent (n = 10) temporary job ended; 8 percent (n = 8) fired; 3 percent (n = 3) drug/alcohol problem; 7 percent (n = 7) prison sentence; 26 percent (n = 27) reported some other reason not listed in the categories provided in the questionnaire.

Although data on family size were collected, a limitation of the study is that it did not collect data on the actual amount of wage earnings. It is assumed in this study that wage earnings are below amounts needed for housing. However, future research should test this hypothesis by accounting for actual earnings and family size and comparing annual earnings with poverty-line income. In addition, it was assumed that most of the homeless were in low-paying service-sector jobs, since industry jobs tend to pay higher wages.

Table 2-1
Frequency Distributions for Gender, Ethnicity, Employment
Status, Age, and Education of Homeless Sample (n = 178)

	Percentage	*Number*
Gender		
Male	55	98
Female	45	80
Ethnicity		
White	48	86
Black	48	85
Other	4	7
Employment		
None	65	116
Part-time	11	19
Full-time	24	43
Age		
16–24	15	26
25–34	40	72
35–44	23	40
45–54	13	23
55–78	8	15
Education		
0–8 grades	8	15
9–11 grades	23	40
High school	42	74
Some college and above	28	49

However, finding the numbers of homeless who are actually in service-sector and industry jobs is an important focus for future research.

Zero-ordered correlations were computed for status of employment with the following variables: gender, ethnicity, age, education, military status, length of homelessness, health, alcohol use, previous mental hospitalization, disability, marital status, and food deprivation (see table 2–2).

Of the twelve variables used in the correlation analysis, six were significant at the .05 level or beyond. The six variables were: gender ($r = .28$); disability ($r = .23$); education ($r = .18$); previous mental hospitalization ($r = .15$); health ($r = .15$); and military experience (veteran) ($r = .14$).

The findings indicate that homeless people who were men, not disabled, relatively better-educated, not previously in a mental hospital, relatively more healthy, and served in the military were more likely to be employed than other homeless people. No differences were found in ethnicity, age, marital status, length of homelessness, food deprivation, and use of alcohol.

In the earlier study, the following were the bivariate results: four of the variables are significantly associated: gender ($x^2 = 16.5548$; phi $= .3049$; $p \leq .001$); disability ($x^2 = 9.4052$; phi $= .2305$; $p \leq .01$); education

Table 2–2
Zero-Ordered Correlations (Pearson's *r*) for Variables
with Employment

	Pearson's r
Gender	.28**
Ethnicity	−.09
Age	−.04
Education	.18*
Military status	.14*
Length of homelessness	−.04
Health	.15*
Alcohol use	−.04
Previous mental hospitalization	.15*
Disability	.23**
Marital status	.08
Food deprivation	−.10
Services and Resource Need	
Affordable housing	−.04
Locating housing	−.11
Job training	−.08
Job finding	−.33**
Educational	−.02
Psychological	−.16*
Medical	−.03
Child care	−.17*
Individual counseling	−.14*
Family counseling	−.13*
Case work advocacy	.04
Social service benefits	−.24*
Parent skill training	−.04
Budget counseling	.08
Food	−.06
Shared living skills	−.01
Alcohol/drug rehabilitation	−.05
Transportation	−.12

*p < .05
**p < .01

(x^2 = 5.9380; phi = .1826; p ≤ .01); and health (x^2 = 3.7561; phi = .1452; p ≤ .05). Consequently, in this second bivariate analysis, two additional variables show significance: previous mental hospitalization and prior military service.

Table 2–3 presents the frequency distributions for service needs of the total sample and for the subgroup of the working homeless.

Subjects identified services and needs that they would find useful by

Table 2–3
Frequency Distributions of Services and Resource Needs of Total Homeless Sample (n = 178) and Employed Homeless (n = 62)

	Total Sample		Employed Homeless	
	Percentage	Number	Percentage	Number
Affordable housing	74	132	73	45
Locating housing	60	107	53	33
Job training	33	59	27	17
Job finding	51	90	30	19
Education	29	52	29	18
Psychological	13	24	7	4
Medical	34	60	32	20
Child care	20	36	10	6
Individual counseling	19	33	11	7
Family counseling	16	29	11	7
Case work advocacy	28	50	31	19
Social service benefits	42	75	27	17
Parent skill training	10	18	8	5
Budget counseling	25	44	27	17
Food	39	69	32	20
Shared living skills	12	21	11	7
Alcohol and drug rehabilitation	14	25	13	8
Transportation	53	95	47	29

responding "yes" or "no" to each item on a list (therefore, each item includes 100 percent of the subjects). The following are the percentages of "yes" responses for each item: 74 percent (n = 132) affordable housing; 60 percent (n = 107) locating housing; 53 percent (n = 95) transportation; 51 percent (n = 90) job finding; 42 percent (n = 75) social service benefits; 39 percent (n = 69) food; 34 percent (n = 60) medical; 33 percent (n = 59) job training; 29 percent (n = 52) education; 28 percent (n = 50) case work advocacy; 25 percent (n = 44) budget counseling; and 20 percent (n = 36) child care (see table 2–3 for those under 20 percent).

The following are "yes" responses for the subgroup of the working homeless (n = 62); 73 percent (n = 45) affordable housing; 53 percent (n = 33) locating housing; 47 percent (n = 29) transportation; 32 percent (n = 20) food; 32 percent (n = 20) medical; 31 percent (n = 19) case work advocacy; 30 percent (n = 19) job finding; 29 percent (n = 18) education; 27 percent (n = 17) social service benefits; 27 percent (n = 17) job training; 27 percent (n = 17) budget counseling (see table 2–3 for those under 20 percent).

Whereas the above distributions indicate the significance of all services (for example, regardless of employment status most homeless subjects were requesting affordable housing), the zero-ordered correlations gave an indication of the variance of needs and services as employment level increased (see table 2–2). While a number of variables showed no significance because of reduced variance in the need, the following five were significant (p ≤ .05) with employment status: job finding ($r = -.33$); social service benefits ($r = -.24$); child care ($r = -.17$); psychological services ($r = -.16$); individual counseling ($r = -.14$); and family counseling ($r = -.13$). The negative correlations indicate that employed subjects requested these services less than unemployed subjects.

The results of the earlier study were: job finding ($x^2 = 15.0937$; phi $= .2912$; p ≤ .0001); child care services ($x^2 = 6.5597$; phi $= 1919$; p ≤ .01); social service benefits ($x^2 = 8.4497$; phi $= .2178$; p ≤ .01); and individual counseling ($x^2 = 4.0323$; phi $= .1505$; p ≤ .05). The two additional variables that show significance in this second study were psychological services and family counseling.

Multivariate Findings

A multivariate design was utilized to analyze the effect of each independent variable, with other variables held constant. Logistic regression procedure was selected because it is especially designed for dichotomous variables and does not require a joint multivariate normal distribution. It examines multiple contingency tables for all possible effects of predictors and indicates which predictors can be ignored, while deriving expected cell values that are minimally different from the observed counts.

Six regression equations are computed because the size of the sample does not permit simultaneous regression of all variables. Regression I evaluates the effect of six demographic variables (see table 2–4 for all regression results). Regression II evaluates the effect of length of homelessness and five health/mental health variables. Regressions III and IV divide the needs and services into groups of nine. The variables that were significant from Regression I and II were regressed on the dependent variable in a single regression (Regression V), and likewise, the needs and services variables that were significant in Regressions III and IV were computed together in Regression VI. Therefore, Regressions V and VI establish an understanding of significant variables when in competition with each other.

The standard T-test for regression coefficients revealed that gender (beta = .9386) and education (beta = .6827) were significant predictors of employment among this homeless sample. Variables that were not significant were: ethnicity, age, marital status, and military status. Regression II (health/mental health variables) shows that among the variables regressed, only disability (beta = .7930) was a significant predictor. Insignificant variables were: length of homelessness, food deprivation, previous mental hospitalization, alcohol use, and health status. Regressions III and IV demonstrated that four needs and services were significant: case advocacy (beta =

Table 2–4
Logistic Regression Results of Variables on Employment Status

Variables	Regression Coefficient	T-test	Probability of Change
Regression I			
Gender	.93868	3.99**	.99
Ethnicity	−.1216	−.65	.16
Age	−.0188	−.10	.03
Education	.6827	2.90**	.73
Military status	−.2559	−1.08	.27
Marital status	.3710	1.31	.34
Regression II			
Length of homelessness	−.0180	−.08	.02
Health	.1494	.65	.16
Alcohol use	.1995	.87	.22
Previous mental hospitalization	.3904	1.12	.28
Disability	.7930	2.52*	.63
Food deprivation	−.2972	−1.26	.32
Regression III			
Affordable housing	.2906	1.19	.30
Locating housing	−.2221	−1.00	.25
Job training	.2127	.92	.23
Job finding	−.7334	−3.37**	.84
Budget counseling	.3489	1.47	.37
Food	−.0815	−.40	.10
Medical	.0524	.25	.06
Child care	−.6657	−2.34*	.59
Transportation	.0832	.39	.10
Regression IV			
Individual counseling	−.3148	.78	.20
Family counseling	−.2174	−.75	.19
Case work advocacy	.4530	2.09*	.52
Social service benefits	−.5760	−2.90**	.73
Parent skill training	−.0621	−.17	.04
Psychological	−.4281	−1.20	.30
Educational	.1772	.78	.20
Shared living skills	.1900	.63	.16
Alcohol/drug rehabilitation	.1648	.60	.15
Regression V			
Gender	.8229	4.40**	1.10
Disability	.7720	3.23**	.81
Education	.5670	2.77**	.69
Regression VI			
Job finding	−.5588	−3.08**	.77
Child care	−.4293	−1.66*	.42
Case work advocacy	.4234	2.05*	.51
Social service benefits	−.3970	−2.06*	.52

*p < .05
**p < .01

.4530), job finding (beta = −.7334), child care (beta = −.6557), and social service benefits (beta = −.5760).

When the significant variables of the first two regressions were computed together in Regression V, all three remained significant predictors: gender (beta = .8339), disability (beta = .7720), and education (beta = .5670). Likewise, when the four significant needs and service variables were computed together in Regression VI, all four remained significant: case advocacy (beta = .4234), job finding (beta = −.5588), child care (beta = −.4293), and social service benefits (beta = −.3970).

The probability of change (PC) column in the regression tables shows the probability of changing from one category of the dichotomous dependent variable to the other, given changes from one category to another in the predictor. These probabilities of change allow us to rank the factors in terms of their additive contribution to the change in probability of employment. Therefore, the strongest predictor of employment is gender, followed by disability and education. The only positive predictor from needs and services is case advocacy. Interestingly, the other three have negative correlations with employment and rank as follows: job finding, social service benefits, and child care.

In summary, the multivariate analysis tell us that those who were employed were more likely to be male, without disabilities, and better-educated than their unemployed counterparts. Additionally, employed homeless individuals were more likely to request case advocacy services than unemployed homeless individuals. They were less likely, however, to request assistance in job finding, social service benefits, and child care.

Discussion

We were surprised to discover that over one-third of the homeless subjects of this study were employed—yet they *were* homeless. Although one-fourth of the subjects were working full-time, they could not afford housing on their full-time wages. Prior to recent times, full-time employment usually guaranteed the worker shelter. We hypothesize that these subjects are victims of economic dislocation.

While the number of working homeless is significant, it is also important to assess the reasons for unemployment. Twenty percent of the subjects stated directly that they lost their former jobs as a result of companies closing or moving or because their temporary jobs ended. However, we suspect this number is under-reported because of a flaw in the categories of the questionnaire. "Fired" and "quit" were two of the choices provided (subjects were only to chose one of ten choices). These two categories do not allow amplification as to the reasons they quit or were fired. For example, approximately one-fourth of the subjects answered that they quit their jobs, and we do not have information on why they quit. While people quit jobs for a variety of reasons, some of the subjects may have quit because of low pay or poor working conditions. Yet some employees may have been forced out of their jobs by employers making situations intolerable. Similarly, those answering "fired" may have been forced out because of economic decisions of the company.

Employment status of homeless individuals was associated with the same structural discrimination workers face in the mainstream economy. That is, discrimination exists against women, people who lack education, and disabled people (findings of the multivariate design), and possibly slight discrimination against those with previous mental hospitalizations and those who are unhealthy, and slight favoritism toward veterans (additional variables significant in the bivariate findings). For example, men, high school graduates, people without health problems and disabilities, and veterans are more likely to be employed than others, regardless if they are homeless or not.

We can increase the number of workers among the homeless by eliminating or reducing the effects of structural discrimination. However, their ability to secure housing remains dismal if the jobs they find are low-paying. Economic dislocation may have affected the majority of homeless people of this study if we include, along with the subjects who were employed at the time of the study, those who were unemployed because of company decisions and were able and willing to work but could not find jobs. Additionally, to some degree, economic dislocation may have played a substantial role in the deteriorating course of personal problems, drug and alcohol addiction, or the mental illness of some subjects to the point that they become not just unemployed, but unemployable. Although we are not at a point in the research process to access and measure the effects of economic dislocation on these conditions, we believe that if those seriously affected also were counted as economically dislocated, we would be able to explain the lion's share of homelessness. In the end, however, some unemployment will continue to persist despite broadening economic opportunities.

Often services are designed by well-intentioned professionals without consulting the target group of their intervention. Gaining information from the homeless is a valuable resource in designing effective services that will meet their needs. The top services requested by the total group of homeless people were ranked in the following order: affordable housing, locating housing, transportation, job finding, social service benefits, food, medical care, job training, education, casework advocacy, and budget counseling. Many of the services requested by the homeless subjects are directly related to survival needs such as shelter and food or services that will allow them to work. This sample of homeless persons is not a group of mentally ill individuals who are unable or unwilling to work. They want services that will allow them to pull themselves out of homelessness. Unfortunately, we believe that individual efforts of the homeless subjects and services that focus only on improving individual deficits will be largely insufficient to resolve the homelessness problem.

Interestingly, all the therapeutic services for mental, emotional, and social problems, such as individual and family counseling, rank lowest among the priorities of the subjects. This finding has several possible explanations or combination of explanations: (1) the mental, emotional and social health of the homeless is not different than the general population; (2) homeless people do not value therapeutic services as a matter of choice or acculturation; (3) the homeless are focused more on the urgency of survival needs than therapeutic needs.

The statistical analyses established those needs and services that vary in relation to employment status. For example, no difference exists with the need for affordable housing because most homeless people request this assistance regardless of employment status. The multivariate analysis revealed that employed subjects tended to request case advocacy services more than unemployed subjects. Perhaps employed homeless persons view themselves as active participants in rising out of homelessness and want assistance that will help them make it on the income they earn. The negative correlations found in job finding, social service benefits, and child care may indicate that employed persons have resolved these issues (for example, since they are employed they do not need assistance in finding a job, their earnings either make them ineligible for social service benefits or they do not want social service benefits, and they have found resources for child care—about one-half of those employed are parents). Conversely, unemployed homeless people need two of the three services (job finding and child care) so that they can work, and they need social service benefits to suffice in the interim.

Interestingly, the bivariate analysis indicated slight negative correlations with mental health services, such as individual and family counseling. Employment may slightly alleviate some of the stress that aggravates family and personal problems. However, overall mental health services were ranked as least desirable by the subjects.

In summation, a large portion of the homeless subjects were either employed at low-paying jobs or unemployed as a result of company economic decisions. The findings lend support to economic dislocation theory as a plausible explanation of homelessness. In addition, services that are most meaningful to the homeless subjects of this study were those services that helped them obtain survival needs and employment.

Implications for Future Research

Although we found that a significant number of people were working yet were homeless, the full impact of economic dislocation has not been revealed. Is economic dislocation a primary factor or an associated variable to homelessness? Do individual strengths play a role in economic recovery of displaced workers? If they do play a role, is that role primary or ancillary?

A problem exists in operationally defining economic dislocation. We have yet to satisfactorily define the variable in a way it can be adequately measured. The study presented in this chapter focused on homeless people who were currently working at the time of the survey. Future research should include these low wage earners with those who lost their jobs because of company decisions. When we added this group to the working homeless subjects, a large percentage of the sample were either working but could not afford housing or were dismissed from their jobs because of company decisions. A large group of respondents reported quitting their jobs, being fired, or losing their jobs for some other reason. However, we were unable to determine to what extent economic dislocation played a part in these responses. Careful investigation into why and how people lose their jobs and index construction for measuring variables should be a major objective of future research. The measurement of degree of economic dislocation is possible if the loss of the job can be evaluated in comparison with other interrelated variables on some continuum. Albeit, decisions of inclusion will at first be based primarily on face validity; other forms of validation are possible as the research advances. For example, if an employee was alcoholic and had warnings for dismissal prior to news of a company's change in status, this person may have lost the position and may have become homeless regardless of the direction taken by the company. Thus, this person could be considered low on a level of economic dislocation. Conversely, high on the scale would be the employee who performed adequately on the job, did not have a history of mental disorders, and lost the job due to company change. The individual factors of adaptability and talents would be the subject of the control variables used in the analysis. As in any attempt to study a relatively unexplored area of social science research, operational definitions take repeated studies to develop reliable and valid measures.

Another approach is to formulate studies that compare victims of economic dislocation that become homeless with those whom do not become homeless. For example, employees of companies who relocate, merge, or consolidate could be followed to find the incidence of homelessness created, while controlling for factors of individual deficits that were evident prior to the employee's awareness of upcoming loss of job. For example, are psychosocial variables of alcoholism and mental disorders evident prior to the change of status, or do they develop after loss of employment? And for those who manifested problems prior to news of the change, has the dislocation produced a deterioration in their condition that disables them from making an economic recovery? What happens to subjects who do not manifest individual deficits in mental status? Do these people become homeless? Some measure of diversity of abilities has to be ascertained. Do employees with several skills or higher levels of adaptability, intelligence, and talent, find employment with adequate wages? We suspect there is a unilateral effect of economic dislocation; however, the least adaptable in terms of skills and other attributes are affected the most.

One of the most notable problems with research on economic dislocation is the probable resistance of companies to any effort that may expose adverse consequences of company actions. Gaining the support of labor unions, government officials, and consumers might help persuade companies to give entry to this research and also could help in developing legislation that would make independent research mandatory. The use of large sample groups involving a number of companies on a highly confidential basis may influence participation.

Later in the process, experimental and quasi-experimental designs are possible to evaluate the effect of certain interventions. For example, if legislation and other interventions were enacted in one city to reduce the effects of economic dislocation, homelessness could be studied prior to enactment and then again after a certain length of time. A city with similar characteristics of the experimental city, yet without the intervention, can be used as a control.

The substance of the types of interventions that can be employed is the focus of the next chapter. The high rate of homelessness compels society to begin active experimentation with alternatives.

Reference

DiBlasio, F.A., Belcher, J. & Connors, C. The working homeless: A crisis in public policy. Unpublished manuscript.

3
Alternatives to Economic Dislocation

The economic dislocation model suggests that efforts to prevent homelessness must be aided at developing effective interventions in the marketplace to influence the decision making of business. This approach, however, involves a delicate balancing act between the interests of capital, the interests of labor, and the ability of the economy to maintain its worldwide competitiveness. Yet achieving a balance between these competing interests is difficult because each interest group frames its view of the problem differently. For example, efforts to increase the minimum wage have sparked controversy over the number of jobs that will ultimately be eliminated. While there is agreement among many that the number of working poor is rising (between 1978 and 1987, over 562,000 more people are working full-time but are still living in poverty), some are concerned that an increase in the minimum wage will result in many of these wage earners losing their jobs and having to be supported by public assistance. The Bush administration has argued that an increase in the minimum wage to $4.65 an hour would result in the loss of 227,000 jobs, whereas the Congressional Budget Office estimates that $4.65 hourly rate would result in the loss of between 125,000 and 250,000 jobs.

On one hand, the estimates overlap and provide a basis for compromise. On the other hand, compromise has generally resulted in incremental change in which the interests of the poor have been sacrificed for the "economic stability" of the nation. It would be naive to suggest broad sweeping changes that significantly undermine the structures of capitalism because in the final analysis, capitalism has enabled this nation to prosper and develop a standard of living, for most, that provides comparatively high worldwide standards of employment, housing, and health care. However, at this point in our nation's history, in which homelessness has reached crisis proportions, continued incremental change will not solve the problem.

In one way or another homelessness is directly related to an individual's or family's inability to afford housing. Instead of this being defined as solely a housing problem, the family must have enough income to be able to both afford and maintain housing. We stress developing higher incomes as opposed to simply housing the poor, for the nation could achieve this latter goal by developing more public housing. Rather than single out the poor, we as a society need to improve everyone's ability to participate in the economic mainstream of society.

A resolution to this crisis depends on the ability of society to simultaneously facilitate ways for individuals to increase income, develop and maintain assets, and regulate the housing industry to maintain fairness. Admittedly, these approaches are direct interventions in the marketplace. They are designed to maintain a market economy and at the same time minimize the risk of economic dislocation to individuals and families. This chapter will focus on methods by which the system can continue to attain high levels of national growth with less homelessness. Interventions in this chapter will focus on income, and chapter 5 will focus on regulating the housing market.

Intervening in the Current Job Market

The first of these approaches, facilitating ways for individuals to increase income, is based on the fact that the employment needs of the economy change in ways that directly determine the ability of individuals to be self-sufficient. Keynesian economic theory has long held that during times of economic sluggishness, increased spending by the federal government would push the economy back into prosperity. However, Keynes failed to judge correctly the monopolistic control exerted over the economy by corporations. As a result, inadequate demand cannot be corrected by increasing the consumer's ability to buy more products. As noted by Alperovitz and Faux (1984):

> All this creates a major problem for Keynesian economics: before a new stream of spending can stimulate new production to hire the unemployed, it regularly gets converted into high prices, wages, profits, and incomes by the more monopolistic sectors of the economy. (p. 35)

The power of the corporation has surpassed the ability of government to control the economy through the traditional practice of using the federal reserve to adjust credit and the money supply. Instead, interventions must more directly affect corporate decision making.

The monopolistic advantage enjoyed by corporations is illustrated by their ability to radically change the employment patterns of the nation with little interference by government. As noted in chapter 1, the switch to a predominantly service-sector economy was no accident. Instead, it was designed to enhance corporate profits. At the same time, manufacturing jobs have significantly declined. Workers, because of lack of information, difficulty in attaining new skills, and lack of mobility, are frequently unable to adjust to the changing employment demands of the job market. Meanwhile, corporations are able to pit worker against worker and obtain lower wage rates.

This has created an interesting phenomenon in which older workers (those 55 and over) who were employed as operators, laborers, and fabricators have often been forced out of the job market. For example, Bethlehem Steel at its Sparrows Point steel mill in Baltimore has eliminated 1,200 full-time jobs over the last three years through a system known as *contracting out* (Burns, 1989). This process enables the company to contract with a firm to provide a specific product for a set price. The contractor often uses temporary workers, who receive low wages and relatively few benefits. Meanwhile, the company is able to reduce spending by not using union labor. Admittedly, many older workers are given the option of accepting early retirement. However, some of these workers are not ready to retire and suffer financial hardship as a result. These individuals frequently find that their standards of living decline, however, many, because of early retirement income, savings, part-time work, already accumulated assets, or a working spouse, are able to avoid homelessness. Although many of these workers have relatively little education, perhaps a high school diploma, they were able to maintain a relatively modest living standard for much of their lives.

On the other hand, the current job market is increasingly being dominated by jobs that require at least one year of college (Silvestri & Lukasiewicz 1987). Most important to note is the sharp decline projected for jobs that require less than a high school degree. Therefore, while the jobs of past decades enabled relatively poorly skilled individuals to avoid poverty and eventual homelessness, the jobs of the late 1980s and 1990s will not. This fact is particularly relevant for the 14 to 25 percent of teenagers who drop out of high school (Finn 1987). Unemployment for these high school dropouts, as adults, particularly black men between the ages of 20 to 24, is over 15.7 percent (Ballen & Freeman 1986).

Given the increasing technological requirements of the job market, high school dropouts and those with less than one year of college will confront increasing difficulty in finding employment. The fact that most studies of the homeless cite a significant number of individuals with less than a high school education is not surprising. However, these studies have only scratched the tip of the iceberg, for there are large numbers of individuals who are unable to find work and live temporarily with their families and friends. These individuals are not generally counted in conventional shelter studies.

In a sense, the continuing increase in high school dropouts and those who do not go on to college, even community college, represents a challenge to those interested in preventing homelessness. Resolving this problem can take two approaches: first, increasing the number of manufacturing jobs in this country so that less-skilled individuals will be ensured employment; and second, increasing the number of people who finish high school and go on to college.

The first approach involves the United States recapturing its competitive advantage by creating new manufacturing jobs and preventing existing manufacturing jobs from being destroyed or exported overseas. One of the drawbacks to this approach is that standards of living in less-developed countries may be potentially damaged as the United States regains its competitive advantage. This will be the subject of discussion in chapter 8. Improving the educational level of this nation's workforce will be the subject of chapter 4. This approach requires reforms in the education system that will increase the likelihood that all children (and particularly poor children) will receive the same education as those in the more affluent classes of society.

Corporate Mistakes Versus Worker Productivity

Approaches to remedy the decline in manufacturing are made difficult by the continuing controversy over why the decline has occurred. Liberal economists, such as Bluestone and Harrison (1982) and Harrison and Bluestone (1988), argue that corporate incompetence and greed and corporations' inability to exploit increasing surplus value from workers led to a situation in which the United States had difficulty competing in world markets. On the other hand, more conservative economists, such as Thurow (1984), blame poor worker productivity and workers' constant demand for higher wages as the cause of the United States being unable to compete in world markets.

Over the last sixty years, the United States economy has moved from a point in its world trade situation in which exports and imports accounted for only 4 to 5 percent of the Gross National Product (GNP) to a situation in which exports and imports account for 13 percent in the 1980s (Thurow 1984). This means that 70 percent of goods and services produced in the United States must compete in the world market. An analysis of the United State's difficulty in competing in world markets may seem far removed from the homeless person wandering the streets. However, homelessness is simply a reflection of the decade-long decline in standards of living for many Americans.

This decline can be directly traced to the fact that during the 1970s, corporate profits declined in response to increasing world competitiveness. For the first time in this nation's history, chief executive officers (CEOs) confronted overseas competition that was beyond their ability to control directly. It is at this point that the two economic camps, liberal and conservative, take different routes in their analyses of the problem.

Liberal economists charge that rather than develop new products that could effectively compete in world markets, CEOs became preoccupied with short-term profits. It is noted, for example, that the average CEO specialized in finance instead of production (Patton 1985). Consequently, the long-term survivability of the corporation was less important than its ability to produce increasing profits. Between 1979 and 1982, corporations spent $170 billion to acquire new companies, and between 1983 and 1984, that amount doubled (Bell 1987). The trend has continued, and corporations have frequently had little capital to invest in new technology or in upgrading aging plant and equipment. Illustrative of this phenomenon, Goodyear Tire and Rubber Company eliminated approximately 4,000 jobs in 1987 in order to generate enough cash to fight off the corporate raider Sir James Goldsmith. The cumulative effect of this siphoning of cash from Goodyear is not yet fully known. However, the long-term ability of the company to invest in updating plant and equipment is doubtful.

As a result, factories continue to age and have often lost their competitive advantage. From this vantage point, the shift to services was the result of corporate mismanagement, fear, corporate *swashbuckling* (a preoccupation with acquiring other corporations as if it were a game), and a lack of long-term investment capital. Another charge by liberal economists is that corporations covered up their diversions of capital into such efforts as fighting off corporate raiders by blaming labor for wanting excessive increases in their wage rates. The much lower wage rates of developing nations is then used to justify the relocation of U.S. corporations overseas.

An often overlooked fact is that workers are only as productive as the machinery or technology that they have at their disposal. However, efficient and updated machinery and technology are dependent upon the ability of the corporation to have sufficient capital to invest. As corporations became more preoccupied with takeovers than the survivability of the companies, the productivity of labor declined.

Conservative economists tend to blame the worker for the demise of U.S. competitiveness and overlook the amount of capital absorbed by corporate mergers and takeovers. They charge that worker productivity has slowed dramatically, from 3 percent a year in 1965 to ½ percent a year in 1984 (Thurow 1984). Therefore, workers' demands for increased wages make U.S. product uncompetitive because the increased wage is not matched by an increase in productivity that could enable corporations to maintain their profit margins without raising prices. Increased prices, it is argued, will place the United States at an unfair disadvantage in world markets.

The supposed decline in worker productivity pales under closer scrutiny. First is the problem of how to measure output. For example, banking output has been said to have declined—yet it is measured according to the number of new individuals employed in this industry (Block 1987). Studies that took into account the investment many banks made in sophisticated computerization and new facilities show that banking productivity rose 6 percent (Brand

& Duke 1983). Obviously, changes in technology and equipment are important to consider in estimating the productivity of a particular industry.

Another related issue is that productivity is highest when output and demand are rising rapidly. Therefore, apparent slowdowns in productivity will be replaced by a decline in the Gross Domestic Product, which is a measure of current demand.

The second problem in examining worker productivity is that since increased productivity depends, in part, on upgrading technology or plant and equipment, the ability of the firm to actually use the technology purchased in their production process is important to analyze. The company may purchase new equipment but be unable to use it because its work force is either too unsophisticated or the technology will not perform the job it was purchased to perform.

Given these problems, it seems obvious that the rate of decline in worker productivity is overestimated. Instead, it is more appropriate to focus on investments, and not only on the rate of investment but on the actual use of each investment. Reich (1983) has observed that companies, such as USX Corporation (for example), engage in *paper entrepreneurialism,* in which assets are purchased and sold solely to increase short-term returns instead of upgrading the firm's long-term profitability.

Rather than view the decline in manufacturing jobs as resulting from declining worker productivity, it is more appropriate to note the failure of U.S. corporations, such as U.S. Steel in Pittsburgh, to invest in new technology and upgrade their plants and equipment, placing them in a position in which their products cannot effectively compete worldwide. Strategies to address this crisis have a direct impact on the number of people who are vulnerable for becoming homeless. Even if the number of individuals who go on to college could be increased, some individuals would still not be capable of absorbing advanced training. For these individuals, manufacturing jobs that employ semi-skilled and unskilled labor are, perhaps, their only viable avenue for gainful employment.

Whereas conservative economists, such as Thurow and Friedman, argue for government to reduce regulation, decrease taxes, and undermine collective bargaining agreements, liberal economists generally call for intervention that influences business decision making. Three strategies come to mind to address this problem: first, government needs to develop a philosophy in which the economy is managed so as to create and maintain the kinds of jobs necessary to avoid poverty and homelessness; second, the federal tax structure needs to be molded so the economy can be more effectively managed; and third, schools of business must be encouraged to change their curricula to reflect a more long-term perspective in business planning. These approaches are interdependent and attempt to balance the need for corporations to manage their own affairs, while at the same time admitting that the government has a responsibility to ensure that corporations are operating for the public good.

The first of these approaches requires the government to refrain from simply being a spectator of the changing job market. Instead, a more active role in determining the mix of jobs in the market is needed to avert increased poverty and homelessness. Unfortunately, federal administrations have generally supported business growth without critically examining the nature of the jobs being created and, more importantly, without taking note of those lost. This is not to suggest that the federal government is ignorant of the changing job scene. On the contrary, the U.S. Department of Labor publishes the *Monthly Labor Review,* in which they regularly report on changes in the types of jobs and the types of workers needed to work in these industries. Not surprisingly, the federal government does not respond to this data by developing appropriate measures to intervene either in favor of changes or to reduce the impact of changes. For example, a company can be influenced to upgrade aging plants and equipment or to engage in research and development for new products if adjustments in the U.S. tax code rewarded this behavior.

Herbert Stein (1989), former chairman of the Council of Economic Advisers, has recommended that the U.S. president sketch out a set of national priorities. The tax code, along with government regulation and new legislation, would then be used to ensure that targeted areas, such as job creation, acrually were molded in the manner outlined by the sketch. Obviously, this approach has some difficulties. Since the president is frequently a wealthy person and is elected, in large part, by the business establishment and middle- and upper-income voters, it is unlikely that the needs of the poor will be addressed. Therefore, it is necessary to mandate that national priorities will be decided in a manner that takes into account the needs of diverse groups.

One method is to have the president accept recommendations about important national priorities from the Council of Economic Advisers, the National Academy of Sciences, the U.S. Chamber of Commerce, and the AFL-CIO. Obviously, these groups will disagree on much and offer different agendas on both the nature of the problems facing the country and appropriate solutions. This can be solved by creating a commission of representatives from these different groups.

The obvious strength of this approach is that commissions are more able than legislators to make tough decisions that the reality of re-election makes difficult. A legislator, for example, is unlikely to recommend that a cap be placed on home ownership interest if their re-election depends, in large part, on the approval of wealthy homeowners. Commission members, for example a member of the National Academy of Sciences, are under no such pressure.

Reaching a consensus among these various groups would be the job of a joint commission consisting of members from each group. While this process is certainly cumbersome, the resulting consensus will be an informed one, able to more realistically address the needs of the nation. Otherwise, national priorities are too often dictated by presidents with little interest in or knowledge of the effects of poverty.

Some economists, such as Friedman (1981), argue that such interventions would negatively affect the ability of business to compete. On the other hand, in order for U.S. capitalism to continue to prosper, it will no longer be possible for corporations to be consumed by short-term profits. As suggested by many business analysts, corporate boards should reward company managers for long-term growth and not short-term profits (Kraus 1980). In addition, the federal tax code could penalize corporations that choose to reward their managers for short-term profits. Otherwise, the business infrastructure will continue to be destroyed, and U.S. corporations' ability to produce and sell products will diminish.

There are several ways the federal government can develop and implement a national policy designed to create and maintain the kinds of jobs necessary to provide housing for the many instead of for the few. One of the most obvious is through the federal tax structure. Corporations have been able to engage in leveraged buy-outs and to accumulate high amounts of debt devices to finance corporate takeovers and mergers because the federal tax code allows them to deduct the interest on the debt and thereby reduce their overall tax liability. One solution would be for the federal tax code to penalize corporations for engaging in this type of behavior by, first, not allowing the interest to be deducted and, second, charging a penalty or a surcharge on these types of transactions. The federal tax code also could reward corporations by allowing them to deduct interest, and even provide a tax rebate, if they invested in new technology or upgraded plants and equipment that proved to either create manufacturing jobs, save manufacturing jobs, or increase competitiveness.

Regulation is also a factor in the ability of corporations to engage in takeovers. For example, pension funds have increasingly become players in corporate takeovers. Over the last decade, pension funds have been able to increase the share of corporate securities they can own. In 1977, 25 percent of pension fund assets were invested in corporate securities, while in the 1960s, only 5 percent were invested in corporate securities (Brand 1989). This has provided corporations with more capital with which to engage in mergers. Besides exposing future as well as current retirees to unreasonable financial risks, the immediate effect on the economy is the elimination of some jobs. This process can be curtailed by requiring pension funds to invest more of their assets in fixed income securities, such as insured certificates of deposit and bonds (not junk bonds) of well-rated corporations.

Also important is to guard against corporations buying back large portions of their outstanding stock. The "roaring 80s" were, in part, stimulated by corporations artificially inflating the market values of their stocks by reducing the number of available shares. This practice, however, has increased their outstanding debt by trading in equity, for which they pay relatively modest dividends and for which they do not have to pay in lean economic times, for debt services in which they *must* pay high interest regardless of whether their companies are profitable. At first glance, this process seems far removed from helping the homeless, but the corporation's inability to service outstanding debt will ultimately lead to it reducing wages and laying off workers.

It is also important to encourage corporations to enter manufacturing or to stay in manufacturing through the sharing of technology. Smaller businesses are at a distinct disadvantage in developing and implementing new technologies because they frequently lack capital or access to capital. To address this problem, states, through their university systems, could cooperatively develop and implement new technologies. For example, the State of Maryland has developed the Maryland Industrial Partnerships program, which fosters relationships between the University of Maryland and small companies so they can produce and implement new technologies. Already, twenty-six companies have taken advantage of the program and have been able to develop new technologies that would otherwise have been prohibitively expensive (Davis-Belcher 1988).

In addition to encouraging corporations to invest in new plant and equipment, it is important to preserve the land available for manufacturing. Several cities have already adopted such policies. For example, Portland, Oregon, has had an industrial protection policy in place since 1981. Baltimore established an industrial protection zone along Key Highway in South Baltimore in 1987 (Rosenthal 1989). In order to prevent industrial land from being taken over by developers in search of sites for condominium and other high-rent housing, cities have used industrial protection zones both to attract new manufacturing and to maintain what already exists. This approach does not need additional revenue. It does, however, require government to set priorities on what kinds of jobs are necessary to develop a homeless-free economy.

Another approach is to use the federal tax code to penalize corporations that choose to reduce the ratio of manufacturing jobs to service jobs within a company. For example, when USX Corporation chose to diversify into oil and reduce its ratio of manufacturing jobs, it would have been charged a penalty under this approach. In addition, firms would no longer be able to take a charge against income when they decided to shut down a plant.

Obviously, allowances would have to be made for corporations to close down plants, but certain criteria would have to be met first. For example, was the plant being closed because it was losing money? If so, could a combination of government loans and supervision return the plant to survivability? If the plant was closed, who would be responsible for taking care of workers displaced by the closure, the company or the federal government? What happens to the current management if the government bails out the corporation? It seems unsound to reward management that has lost money by bailing them out. Therefore, one condition for a government bail-out would be that the current management would be replaced. These questions need to be resolved before a plant may shut down. Otherwise, corporations may engage in practices that are in their best interest but are negative for the overall economy.

It would also be necessary to reduce the number of firms that relocate by increasing the cost to corporations considering a relocation. Plant relocations and plant closures are very costly to workers and to local governments; however, business is seldom asked to pay for these costs. As a result, business decisions are made as if there were no cost involved. For example, when the Youngstown Sheet and Tube Works closed in the late 1970s, tax collections dropped by 40 percent and unemployment rose to 10 percent (Alperovitz & Faux 1984).

The notion of assessing business for the *true* cost of a corporate relocation still enables a business to make its own decisions. However, the business is no longer able to make its decisions as if only it were affected by the decision. It is doubtful that some businesses would choose to move if they had to pay for the total cost of the relocation.

Finally, the government could shift some of its massive research and development efforts from other areas, such as defense, and concentrate on the development of new products. This technology could then be sold to corporations at a reduced cost, and the corporation would be required to manufacture the product and not sell the technology to another company or country. The government also could invest in upgrading the infrastructure of the country in such a way that manufacturing was encouraged. For example, the nation's aging port facility system could be upgraded, which would require products from heavy industry and provide jobs. This investment also would enhance the nation's ability to compete worldwide. On the other hand, the same investment in a tank or aircraft carrier may create jobs, but the tank will not spawn as many permanent jobs or as much industry.

Further examples of how an investment in the infrastructure will create jobs include fixing deteriorating bridges, which would create 100,000 new jobs (U.S. Department of Transportation 1981) and repair and new construction of waste water treatment facilities, which would create 250,000 new jobs (Choate and Walter 1981). It should be noted that while these figures are somewhat dated, there has been no significant repair of the infrastructure. In fact, neglect by the Reagan administration has created a situation in which vast numbers of workers could be employed at rebuilding the infrastructure.

The third approach would be to influence the nation's business schools to alter their curricula to reflect the teaching of a more balanced approach to investment. Not to impinge on academic freedom, this teaching would not have to take place at the expense of other scholarship, such as Milton Friedman's, a noted conservative economist. However, universities that wanted federal grant money would have to demonstrate that their curriculum reflected a balanced approach toward investment. In particular, it is important that business schools point out that a market-driven economy has weaknesses as well as strengths. Thus the conventional free-market (let the buyer beware) philosophy would be taught alongside philosophies such as socialism and a mixed economy approach that challenge conventional wisdom.

Thus far, we have outlined some methods for addressing the decline in manufacturing jobs. Despite the best efforts of these approaches, it is doubtful that the United States will regain the large number of manufacturing jobs that once characterized this nation. The fact that other countries, such as Japan, have established a competitive edge in such industries as automobile production suggests that the regaining of U.S. competitiveness will be difficult. In the meantime, the dearth of manufacturing jobs must be addressed by educating individuals who are able to be employed by the higher-paying portions of the services industry.

Jobs in the Central Cities

Economic opportunity is directly related to the availability of jobs that enable individuals to be self-sufficient. The creation of such jobs in central cities has too often been left to chance. The federal government has failed to mandate that contractors who are awarded government contracts locate a certain percentage of their facilities in central cities. However, government contractors are allowed to develop new production facilities in locations that are for the companies' convenience as opposed to locations, such as central cities, where the jobs are needed.

Once again, our nation's central cities could benefit from significant investment in their infrastructures. Not only would this represent an investment in the renewal of the economy because firms will be able to get their products to market, but needed jobs would be created. Otherwise, the years of neglect to the infrastructure of central cities will mean that they become vast wastelands.

In addition, tax incentives could be designed to encourage industry to locate and remain in central cities. These efforts alone, however, may not be enough to encourage corporations to locate in central cities. In these instances, the federal government will need to use some form of revenue-sharing to enable cities to employ targeted individuals in city jobs. Interestingly, this was once done under the rubric of Federal Revenue Sharing Funds and the Comprehensive Employment and Training Act (CETA). City governments benefited, particularly those with insufficient tax bases, because they were able to perform basic city services. However, the Reagan administration dramatically changed the relationship between the federal government and the central cities. This redefinition has increased pressure on local governments to curtail employment training and reduce the number of city employees.

Instead of focusing on the need for federal dollars to bring about changes in central cities, Reagan focused on the private sector. In addition, no rules or specific expectations were attached to these efforts. The Committee for Economic Development (1982) summarizes the view characteristic of Reaganomics and development in inner cities:

> Indeed, the entrepreneurial thrust of business . . . may well be indispensable in achieving a permanent solution to urban and other socio-economic problems that have badly overtaxed the capacity of public agencies. (p. 10)

The Reagan era's emphasis on growth through economic development was important; however, by not mandating the kinds of efforts expected from business and by excluding fiscal participation by the federal government, the proposal was like a lifeboat with no bottom. The next several years under President Bush will probably be more of the same. The Center on Budget and Policy Priorities, referring to Bush's budget (February 17, 1989), observes:

> [T]he budget's combination of modest domestic initiatives, substantial domestic program cuts, and the capital gains tax cut would be likely to widen the gap between both the wealthy and the poor and the gap between the wealthy and middle class. (pp. 1–2)

An alternative approach would be to mandate expectations to business, such as a requirement that federal contractors locate a certain percentage of their facilities in central cities. In addition, instead of domestic program cuts, there needs to be a greater infusion of money by the federal government through the reestablishment of programs such as CETA.

In addition to efforts to require federal contractors to locate in central cities, a broader-based approach is necessary. Any such approach must take into account that business has the upper hand in situations involving corporate relocations and that central cities, because of their inadequate tax bases, are at a distinct disadvantage in being able to influence these decisions. Fairness can only come about if tax incentives at the local level are made illegal. Instead, plant relocations should be influenced by the federal government, which can take into account the changing needs of different regions. For example, unemployment in certain sections of Chicago means that it would be unwise to allow a plant to relocate from Chicago to a town in North Carolina, where wages and unemployment are lower. Therefore, public policy, through the federal tax code, could be designed to reward a firm for remaining in Chicago and punish them, through a tax surcharge, if they decided to relocate to North Carolina.

Important in any program to revitalize the central cities and increase opportunities for its residents is to encourage corporate investment. While it is relatively easy to prevent companies from leaving an area, it is more difficult to create the kind of business climate in which corporations believe it is profitable to invest. It is important to note that we are not recommending that central cities attempt to lure corporations to relocate through taxes and fiscal inducements. Wasylenko (1981), who has studied geographical relocation decision making by business over the last 20 years, notes:

> Taxes and fiscal inducements have very little, if any affect on industrial location decisions. Thus, state and local policies designed to attract business are generally wasted government resources, since businesses that ultimately locate in that jurisdiction would have made the same decision with or without the fiscal incentive. (p. 56)

On the other hand, central cities that have ignored the needs of businesses that might want to relocate have suffered negative consequences. Schmenner (1980) observes:

> A company may find clues about a community's willingness to host industry by its willingness to grant tax and financial incentives. Industry may find these programs to be mere tokens, insignificant compared with other influences on locations, but they are tokens, nonetheless. The community that actively disdains such incentives, especially the more mundane programs affecting location, may do so at its own peril. (pp. 446–48)

As already noted, it is unfair to less-advantaged communities to allow more prosperous communities to offer tax incentives and financial incentives to attract corporate investors. For example, a city with a limited tax base, such as Baltimore, would face severe economic hardship. One method states frequently try, especially southern states, is to implement right-to-work statutes. These laws make it difficult for unions to organize, and thus prevailing wage rates are generally lower than states were unions are more active.

This process has obvious negative effects on workers because it encourages business to locate in areas where they are best able to determine wage rates that workers are generally unable to effectively challenge. Admittedly, wages and benefits make up a significant portion of a corporation's liabilities. An often overlooked fact, however, is the cost of capital. Currently, corporations depend in large part on the private sector to raise funds. An alternative approach would be to target geographical areas in the country that are suffering high unemployment rates and use loans financed by the U.S. Treasury to encourage business to invest and develop facilities within these targeted areas. Critics, such as the U.S. Chamber of Commerce, will quickly charge that this approach unfairly competes with private banking interests and creates a larger and more unmanageable welfare state. While it is true that this approach does create competition with private banking interests, it needs to be noted that this competition will benefit society by lowering the incidence of poverty.

U.S. Treasury notes and other federal obligations are sold to the public and compete with banks and money market funds by providing investors with alternatives. As a result, interest rates are tied in some way to the auction of federal obligations. Other forms of competition include Veteran Administration (VA) and Federal Housing Administration (FHA) loans. All these forms of competition also benefit banks because they are able to expand their customer base as they sell, broker, service, and purchase these financial devices.

The purpose of this competition is to add stability to the marketplace and, in the case of VA and FHA loans, enable targeted individuals to participate in the mainstream economy. A VA or FHA loan makes it more likely that individuals will one day use a conventional mortgage to purchase their next home.

Our analogy shows that as the government creates opportunities for more investors to enter the marketplace, private banking interests actually increase their potential pool of available customers. If the government selected a particular geographical area, such as the Lawndale section of Chicago, to receive low-interest development loans, one of the effects would be that demand would increase for banking services, such as payroll, consumer loans, and operating capital loans.

Our preferences to stimulate growth through the creation of capital is based on the premise that workers must earn enough to buy back the goods they produce. This view is not new. In fact, Henry Ford argued that workers had to be paid enough to both maintain their health and also buy back the products they produced. Harrington (1986) points out that Ford wanted to rely on voluntary cooperation by business to achieve the goal of a well-paid work force.

Ford's approach failed, as have most attempts to have business voluntarily regulate itself. As opposed to many Western European countries, such as Sweden, that have a long history of collective responsibility in which the interests of all citizens, rich and poor, are considered important, principles of utilitarianism dominate the American experience. Therefore, it is unlikely that a corporation is going to engage in practices for the greater good unless it is compelled to do so by some outside force, such as the federal government.

Efforts designed to stimulate job growth and rebuild decaying central cities are important. However, unless they are augmented by a method in which the poor are able to develop and maintain assets, it is doubtful that the living standards of the poor will rise.

How to Help the Poor Develop and Maintain Assets

Thus far, much of our discussion has focused on jobs; however, attention needs to be paid to the ability of the poor and near poor to be able to accumulate and maintain assets. In the end, it is one's savings that may prevent one from falling into homelessness. Certain events, such as divorce, major illness, unemployment, disability, and evictions, place the near poor at risk for becoming homeless. The fact that budgets of the poor and near poor are expended so rapidly is not surprising. In 1983, for example, low-income renters paid over 30 percent of their income for rent (General Accounting Office 1985). As already noted, by 1987, it was estimated that low-income renters were paying as much as 50 percent. Because low-income individuals and families must often live in high-crime areas, they must spend additional percentages of their income on protecting what little assets they do have (Sherraden 1988).

As noted in chapter 1, people generally fall into the "near poor" category because of their inconsistent and low incomes. One of the ways society has tried to augment the low wages of the poor is through federally subsidized efforts that focus on rent vouchers. The middle class also enjoys a federally subsidized housing supplement. For example, one of the major ways middle-income buyers are able to purchase homes is by deducting from their tax bill a portion of the interest they pay to finance their homes. This deduction acts to shelter a portion of their income from taxes and also enables them to maintain assets. In 1986, this cost the American taxpayers $44 billion, and 70 percent of these benefits were paid to individuals whose *adjusted gross income* was over $30,000 (Hartman 1987).

Other ways the federal government subsidizes the middle class and the wealthy is by not taxing employer contributions to an employee's health insurance. In 1985, the Council of Economic Advisers estimated that the government subsidized 40 percent of these contributions (1985 Economic Report). Nevertheless, in 1987, 37 million Americans of working age went without health insurance (Wiener 1988–89).

It is obvious that the current set of tax incentives favor the middle and upper classes over the poor and near poor. Rather than comment on the unfairness of these approaches, it seems more important to emphasize that the government has chosen to support more wealthy groups in their efforts to accumulate wealth. The near poor and the poor, on the other hand, are simply left exposed to the indignities of unemployment, sickness, and inadequate retirement pensions. Important in any effort to prevent homelessness is a way of reducing the economic vulnerability of the near poor and poor. A focus on jobs and education will help lessen some of this vulnerability, however, it is also important to ensure that the poor, much like the middle class, are able to develop and maintain assets.

This can take place in three ways: first, there should be a mandate that businesses provide health insurance for their employees, and government should expand Medicaid to unemployed individuals; second, government should subsidize a savings system for the poor and near poor; and third, government should provide for the conversion of rent subsidies to home ownership subsidies. These approaches work together to prevent asset insecurity.

The mandating of health insurance is presently being haphazardly implemented by Section 89 of the Internal Revenue Code (Gutman 1988). This provision requires that companies providing health insurance for some of their employees provide it for *all* their employees. Otherwise, those employees who receive the health insurance must pay taxes on the contribution from the employer. Not surprisingly, companies are simply paying their executives more money to cover the higher taxes in order to avoid extending coverage to other workers. A coalition of interest groups, including the U.S. Chamber of Commerce and other business groups, was able to pressure Congress to overturn retroactively Section 89 on November 13, 1989. As a result, employers are free to offer no health insurance to their employees. In the meantime, millions of employed Americans receive no health insurance, and their salaries make them ineligible for Medicaid. The U.S. Chamber of Commerce has suggested allowing individuals with incomes between 100 and 150 percent of the federal poverty level to purchase, for a sliding-scale premium, primary coverage through Medicaid. It is understandable why business groups want Medicaid to supply health insurance coverage for individuals who are working but who have no health coverage. However, this approach places a greater burden on the federal treasury and absolves business from responsibility. A more equitable approach is to mandate that business provide health insurance to all employees. Critics may charge that this unfairly penalizes businesses; however, business benefits from this approach because it can depend on a more healthy workforce.

The second approach would enable poor and near poor individuals to save money by offering a cash incentive (for example, a tax rebate of ten cents for every dollar invested, even if they owed no tax) for each dollar of savings held over one year, and by not taxing savings for individuals who earn less than $20,000 a year. Obviously, this approach will prove costly to the federal government. Nevertheless, it recognizes that the tax system can be used to subsidize the poor as well as the wealthy. More important, it offers an incentive for poor families to save and thereby set up an economic cushion to prevent homelessness during times of economic dislocation.

Admittedly, the poor are generally trying to survive, and the notion of saving as they struggle through their hand-to-mouth existence appears somewhat far-fetched. However, it should be noted that the overall thrust of the reforms we have suggested are designed to raise many of the poor out of poverty. Therefore, as many of the poor rise from poverty, there need to be methods in which their savings can be augmented through the federal tax system. For example, the federal tax system would be used as an incentive so the poor could shelter their increasing incomes from taxation.

The notion of "making work pay" has been discussed in depth by Ellwood (1988). Basically, Ellwood, along with others such as Wilson (1984), argues that the working poor need to be transformed into role models to show other poor people that it is possible to escape poverty. The federal government already uses the Earned Income Tax Credit (EITC) to provide an added refundable cash incentive for working poor families. In order to qualify, an individual must be employed and have children.

The EITC in 1989 provided a 14 cent credit for each dollar earned up to $6,500. Even if a family owes no taxes, they still can receive a check. As of early 1989, there were several bills before Congress to expand the dollar amount refundable to poor working families. As already suggested, the federal government could provide a credit for every dollar saved. For example, taxpayers could avoid paying taxes on the first $500 of interest received. Unfortunately, this approach would only benefit those who paid taxes. Another approach would be to model the savings incentive program after the EITC program so that the poor could receive benefits even if they paid no taxes.

We have devoted chapter 5 to an in-depth discussion of a more rational housing policy. However, housing is also a form of savings, and a discussion of it is also appropriate in this section. The third approach recognizes the fact that rent subsidies are designed to benefit landlords as much as they benefit the poor people living in the apartments. The landlords might not have as much demand for their rental units and would realize a smaller profit if rent subsidies were reduced. On the other hand, the poor and near poor are denied access to the housing market, and since their apartments do not appreciate, they are denied a form of savings. An alternative is to redefine some of the rent subsidies into housing subsidies so the poor and near poor could take their subsidies and purchase homes. In this way, they could begin to develop and maintain assets. As a result, vulnerability to homelessness would be lessened because even if foreclosure took place, they would probably realize some savings (appreciation) that they could use to avoid homelessness.

Inadequate Welfare Payments and Full Employment

Finally, any comprehensive package designed to alleviate poverty must address the need for adequately funded entitlement programs. We believe that the thrust of any effort to raise people out of poverty should focus on rebuilding the nation's industrial sector. However, some individuals are unable to work and must be supported by the federal government. The only way to raise these people out of poverty is to ensure that entitlements provide a decent income. Rather than detail the reductions in entitlement programs that have taken place during the Reagan years, it seems sufficient to say that entitlement programs, such as Aid to Families with Dependent Children (AFDC) and Supplemental Social Security Income (SSI), should be funded so payments are indexed to the cost of living. Obviously, this involves establishing federal standards, since states currently set their own standards. Also important is a federally mandated cost of living adjustor so, for example, payments in Mississippi would be lower than in New York, however, payments in Mississippi would be based on the actual cost of living for that region.

The notion that the federal government should create jobs is based on the premise that full employment is both healthy for the economy and produces a necessary social good. The alternative to full employment is, as the United States does at present, to use welfare to temporarily assist some unemployed (those who qualify). Piven and Cloward (1971) note, however, that the primary reason for such assistance is to continue the status quo and to keep the poor from rioting. This is because the payments are so low that they generally keep unemployed individuals from starving, but do not enable them to actually make a life for themselves.

There are many ways to achieve full employment: First, using shorter work days and shorter work weeks; second, using government jobs; and third, requiring that businesses maintain their work forces, even in poor economic times. Shorter work days and weeks have been tried in France, however, as Harrington (1986) points out:

> [I]t is absurd to think that the employers of the United States will—or; to be fair, in some cases can—absorb the rapid increase in the hourly wage that would result from requiring them to pay forty hours worth of money for thirty-five hours of work. (p. 151)

The mistake the French made is obvious. An alternative approach is for the federal government to subsidize the employee's lost wages that result from working less than a forty-hour week. This will create fewer hardships for corporations, and their demand for workers will increase because they will need more workers as the result of their workers working fewer hours. What about the cost to the U.S. Treasury? Some of the cost for this program will be paid for by those additional workers who will be paying taxes. There will still be some out-of-pocket costs to the federal government, yet more workers will be employed and will be paying taxes. It should be noted that unemployment is also costly. For example, unemployment creates more crime, drug and alcohol abuse, and a variety of other social problems.

The second approach is to create federal jobs, for example, to rebuild the infrastructure such as the harbor system. These jobs would provide living wages and benefits such as health insurance and retirement. Federal job programs have never been welcomed in this country. Even during the 1930s, a time of high unemployment, there was a widespread fear that these jobs would compete with private industry. Another fear was that individuals who worked for the public sector would become lazy and inefficient. A federal job program should recognize that full employment is desirable, and the government should take steps to ensure its implementation. Government jobs do not, however, have to compete with private industry.

Works Progress Administration (WPA) jobs, during the 1930s, employed individuals in jobs that proved useful to the community. Yet at the same time, the pay was low enough that when a job in private industry became available, the person usually left WPA employment. What about the fact that WPA-type jobs create wage inflation? It is certainly true that in order to lure away workers from the WPA-type jobs, private industry will have to pay higher wages. On the other hand, the benefit to society is obvious: wages will be higher and will hopefully enable more individuals to afford to support a family.

Under this approach, a federally mandated minimum wage is not needed because jobs created by the WPA or similar approach will set a minimum floor on wages. The relevant question for consideration is what the effect of this wage inflation will be on the economy. Obviously, increased wages will create a shortage of goods, and higher prices will follow. However, the relevant issue for discussion is the ability of the government to prevent higher prices without increasing the unemployment rate. In the past, this country has used interest rates to slow down an overheated economy (the notion is that inflation results from too many dollars chasing too few goods, hence an overheated economy). For example, President Ford was very concerned with inflation, so much so that he choked off the economy, and unemployment rose to over 9 percent.

The social cost of the additional unemployment needed to slow down the economy is, in our estimation, simply too high. Increased unemployment creates increased poverty and raises one's vulnerability to becoming homeless. Wage and price controls have generally been ineffective because as soon as they are removed, prices increase to an undesirable level. On the other hand, government could perpetually maintain low prices. However, this has tended to bankrupt a nation's treasury as it must buy some goods and services from overseas, where prices are not being artificially controlled.

Monetarists such as Milton Friedman argue that too much money chasing too few goods leads to inflation. Therefore, much like in the 1981–82 recession created by the Reagan administration, the monetarists argue that the money supply has to be curtailed. The Federal Reserve increases its discount rate, interest rates rise, the economy slows down, and inflation declines. As already noted, the cost of this approach is massive unemployment and homelessness.

Another approach is to develop a more progressive tax system that will in turn slow down the economy because consumers, since they have less disposable income, will purchase less. The increased revenues could be used to enhance the infrastructure and provide more basic services, such as medical care. As consumers decide to spend less, the economy will in turn slow down, creating some unemployment. Given the fact the United States is a consumer-oriented economy, some unemployment will have to be generated to combat inflation. However, the use of tax rates as the primary means to combat inflation should lower the amount of unemployment necessary. Important to note is that the use of tax rates to slow down spending will impinge most dramatically on the upper-income brackets. In addition, those workers who are laid off will be able to maintain their incomes through more generous unemployment compensation. The rising revenues resulting from increasing marginal tax rates would be used to pay unemployment compensation to those workers negatively affected by the slow-down in the economy. The unemployment compensation would be indexed to inflation and pegged to 80 percent of the person's previous wages. As discretionary income decreases, spending will slow down, and the economy should be able to correct itself.

New approaches designed to slow down an overheated economy must recognize that any sacrifice must be made by those individuals with the most income. Workers displaced as the result of the tightening of the economy would receive unemployment compensation that would enable them to avoid economic dislocation. In effect, we are still addressing inflation by slowing down spending. However, our approach cushions the shock caused by the process of inflation reduction. This approach has not been attempted in the United States, perhaps because the cost of fighting inflation has historically been borne by the poor, near poor, and lower-income workers.

There is a further alternative that will reduce the necessity of creating some unemployment. Currently, because our society is consumer-oriented, demand is adversely affected by the consumer's appetite for new goods and the consumer's ability to pay for those goods. This process inherently leads to cycles of inflation, recession, and recovery. An alternative approach would be to change the orientation of society toward creating more social goods, such as parks and theaters. Demand for these products is not based on income, and the economy would not be as subject to inflation and recession.

Financing

Given the large federal deficit created, in large part, by the supply-side tax policies of the Reagan administration, any additional financing to combat homelessness, such as through the approaches we have suggested, will require additional federal fund outlays and corresponding increases in revenues. However, some of what we have suggested will finance itself. The tax penalties suggested to deter corporate mergers, takeovers, and leveraged buy-outs will be self-supporting. Many of the tax incentives used to enable corporations to deduct interest on the purchase of new plants and equipment will offset these revenue enhancers. However, the net effect to the federal treasury should not be significant. Since the tax policies outlined, including the penalty for plant relocation, are designed to maintain or create jobs, the overall effect on the budget should be to increase tax receipts.

Our efforts to improve the nation's economy will inevitably require additional federal fund outlays. Obviously, these outlays will in turn place pressure on the already high federal budget deficit. Unlike the Congressional Budget Office, we will not project an unrealistic level of economic growth. (For example, they have estimated that the economy will grow at a steady rate of 2½ percent a year) or a decline in long-term interest rates. These projections are both overly optimistic and minimize the need for revenue enhancers. Four options have been suggested to raise additional revenues, raise income tax rates, broaden the income tax base, impose a broad consumption tax, and increase excise taxes (Mann & Schultze 1988–89). Given the inherent political difficulties in these options (U.S. taxpayers seem loath to tax increases), one could choose the path of least resistance and opt for an increase in excise taxes, such as a tax on gasoline. Of course, a consumption and an excise tax are regressive and would punish the poor by increasing taxes on their already meager incomes. It seems more appropriate to increase income taxes from their current high of 28 percent to a high of somewhere around 40 to 50 percent. An increase of just one percentage point in personal and corporate income tax would raise approximately $24 million in increased revenues (Aaron 1988–89). In addition, this would raise taxes on those who could best afford it.

Another alternative, which is also a tax increase, is to make current deductions, such as home mortgage interest, more progressive. For example, currently there is no limit on the amount of interest that can be deducted on a primary residence. This system rewards those who can afford to purchase more expensive homes because their interest deductions are subsidized by all taxpayers. Therefore, in theory, a low-income individual must pay higher taxes so the government can allow a more wealthy individual to deduct the interest payments on their principle residence. An alternative is to place a limit on the amount of interest that can be deducted. Obviously, this may reduce sales of higher-priced homes. However, if higher-priced homes result in others going without a home or living in poverty, then the social cost of limitless interest deductions for home mortgage interest is too high.

Are there drawbacks to this proposal? Obviously, an increase in personal income taxes, specifically on more wealthy individuals, will shift the economic balance in America. A decrease in standards of living for more wealthy individuals will occur as the result of our proposals. Some may also argue that the wealthy are the backbone behind the formation of investment capital. Any raising of their tax rates will lessen their ability to invest. The Reagan administration attempted to address this issue by reducing tax rates for the wealthy. The assumption was that the wealthy would take these additional moneys and invest them. However, the current low rate of savings cannot be used as an argument to justify the notion that low tax rates for the wealthy stimulate investment. It is, after all, continued investment that enables the economy to grow and produce more jobs.

Making the tax system into a more progressive one has three strengths: it discourages inflation; it decreases the potential for unrest; and it enables people to avoid the indignities of poverty. Titmus (1965) and Galbraith (1987) have both warned that too much wealth in the hands of a few (as is the case currently in the United States) leads to overall inflation because of speculation. As already noted, it is important for most citizens, particularly those on fixed and limited incomes, to keep inflation to a minimum. Otherwise, the government will be tempted to use monetary policies to combat inflation and create unemployment in the process.

The growing gap between rich and poor is not healthy for the long-term stability of any society. All one has to do is visit Washington D.C. for a graphic example of this phenomenon. Many of the residents of Washington are below the poverty level and unable to obtain gainful employment. There are also sections of Washington in which the wealthy prosper. One result of this imbalance is a crime rate that threatens to throw the city into chaos.

The final reason for a more progressive tax system is that the government would be able to provide more opportunities so more people can avoid poverty. An end result of poverty is homelessness; therefore, one of the major ways to reduce homelessness is through the reduction of poverty.

Conclusion

Ultimately, the choice to influence business decision making and create a more progressive tax system is up to the American electorate; increasing numbers of homeless can be tolerated or efforts can be made to resolve the crisis. Either way will be painful, yet current efforts, such as voluntarism, place most if not all of the suffering on the homeless. The second approach broadens responsibility for resolving the problem to a wider base of the electorate.

While efforts to increase the number of manufacturing jobs, prevent the further decline of the ones remaining, raise the hope and education level of central city youth, and create jobs in inner cities are important, these are long-term solutions, and in the meantime homelessness will continue to grow. It took perhaps ten years or more to create the economic dislocation that is pervasive in this nation, and academic debates will provide little solace to those who are unemployed, underemployed, and already homeless.

Our efforts to avoid short-term solutions are based on the fact that these solutions will simply legitimize homelessness and poverty and further discourage efforts aimed at resolving the problem. The dilemma, of course, is that over the short-term, the homeless have to be sheltered and fed, for we are not suggesting that the immediate needs of the homeless should be ignored. Yet people responsible for current relief efforts need to realize that more shelters are not a solution. Instead, they are a temporary, simplistic, and inadequate way of addressing a long-term and complex crisis.

Our next chapter focuses on needed changes in education that will enable more Americans to participate in the economic mainstream and avoid homelessness.

References

Aaron, H.J. (1988–89). Tax increases: Choosing among four broad options. *The Brookings Review, 7*, (1): 12–13.

Alperovitz, G. & Faux, J. (1984). *Rebuilding America*. New York: Pantheon Books, 147–8.

Baker, N.C. (1989). Would you hire them? *Nation's Business, 77*, (4): 16–29.

Ballen, J. & Freeman, R.B. (1986). Transitions between employment and nonemployment. In Freeman, R.B. & Holzer, H.J. (eds.), *The Black Youth Employment Crisis*. Chicago: National Bureau of Economic Research.

Bell, W. (1987). *Contemporary Social Welfare, 2nd Ed.* New York: MacMillan.

Block, F. (1987). Rethinking the political economy of the welfare state. In Block, F., Cloward, R.A., Ehrenreich, B. & Piven, F.F. (eds.), *The Mean Season: The Attack on the Welfare State*. New York: Pantheon Books.

Bluestone, B. & Harrison, B. (1982). *The Deindustrialization of America*. New York: Basic Books, Inc.

Brand, H. & Duke, J. (1983). Productivity in commercial banking: Computers spur the advance. In U.S. Bureau of Labor Statistics, *A BLS Reader on Productivity*. Washington, D.C.: Government Printing Office, 58–66.

Brand, H. (1989). Merger mania and economic decline. *Dissent*, Spring, 137–42.

Burns, M.K. (1989). Union challenges Bethlehem Steel, other plants on cost-cutting labor practices. *The Baltimore Sun*, April 9, B1.

Center on Budget and Policy Priorities (1989). Bush domestic budget cuts deeper than first reported, new analysis shows. Washington, D.C.: Center on Budget and Policy Priorities, February 17.

Choate, P. & Walter, S. (1981). *America in Ruins: Beyond the Public Works Pork Barrel*. Washington, D.C.: The Council of State Planning Agencies.

Committee for Economic Development (1982). *Public Private Partnership: An*

Opportunity for Urban Communities. New York: Committee for Economic Development.

Davis-Belcher, P. (1988). Grants help companies to do business. *Maryland Agenda, 3,* (June 3): 1, 8.

Economic Report of the President (1985). Washington, D.C.: Government Printing Office.

Ellwood, D. (1988). *Poor Support: Poverty in the American Family*. New York: Basic Books, Inc.

Finn, C.E., Jr. (1987). The high school dropout puzzle. *The Puzzle Interest,* (Spring): 3–22.

Friedman, M. (1981). *Free to Choose: A Personal Statement*. New York: Avon Books.

Galbraith, J.K. (1987). The 1929 parallel. *The Atlantic Monthly,* January, 62–6.

General Accounting Office (1985). *Homelessness: A Complex Problem and Federal Response*. Gaithersburg, Md: U.S. General Accounting Office, GAO/HRD-85-40.

Gutman, L.R. (1988). Warning: Ignoring new benefits can be hazardous to your company's health. *The Maryland Agenda,* (3): 1.

Harrington, M. (1986). *The Next Left*. New York: Henry Holt and Company.

Harrison, B. & Bluestone, B. (1988). *The Great U-Turn: Corporate Restructuring and the Polarizing of America*. New York: Basic Books, Inc.

Hartman, C. (1987). The housing part of the homelessness problem: In *Homelessness: Critical Issues for Policy and Practice*. Boston: The Boston Foundation.

Kraus, D. (1980). Executive Pay: Ripe for reform? *Harvard Business Review,* (Sept–Oct): 36–8.

Mann, T.E. & Schultze, C.L. (1988–89). Getting rid of the budget deficit: Why we should and how we can. *The Brookings Review, 7,* (1): 3–22.

Patton, A. (1985). Why corporations overpay their underachieving bosses. *Washington Post,* March 3, A12.

Piven, F.F. and Cloward, R.A. (1971). *Regulating the Poor, the Functions of Public Welfare*. New York: Pantheon Books, Inc.

Reich, R. (1983). *The Next American Frontier*. New York: Time-Life Books.

Rosenthal, D. (1989). Business battle condo-mania. *The Baltimore Sun,* August 13, E1.

Schmenner, R.W. (1980). *Making Business Location Decisions*. Englewood Cliffs, New Jersey: Prentice-Hall.

Sherraden, M.W. (1988). Rethinking social welfare: Towards assets. *Social Policy, 18,* 37–43.

Silvestri, G.T. & Lukasiewicz, M. (1987). A look at occupational employment trends to the year 2000. *Monthly Labor Review, 110,* (9): 46–63.

Stein, H. (1989). Governing the $5 trillion economy. *The Brookings Review, 7,* (2): 16–23.

Thurow, L.C. (1984). A world class economy. *Tocqueville Review, 6,* 303–26.

Titmus, R.M. (1965). The role of redistribution in social policy. *Social Security Bulletin, 28,* June: 14–32.

U.S. Department of Transportation (March, 1981). Second annual report to Congress on highway and bridges replacement and rehabilitation. Washington, D.C.: Government Printing Office.

Wasylenko, M. (1981). The location of firms: The role of taxes and fiscal incentives. In Bahl, R. (ed.), *Urban Government Finance: Emerging Trends.* Beverly Hills: Sage Publications.

Wiener, J.M. (1988–89). Taking care of the uninsured. *The Brookings Review, 7,* (1):32–3.

Wilson, W.J. (1984). Cycles of deprivation and the underclass debate. *Social Service Review, 12,* 541–559.

4
Educational Reform to Prevent Homelessness

T he least adaptable to the effects of economic dislocation are the poorly educated, who usually qualify for only the service-sector jobs, which pay low wages that do not keep pace with the rising costs of housing. If they are hired and trained in manufacturing positions, they run the risk of job loss because of technological advances and company mergers or relocations. Part of the equation to minimize the impact of economic dislocation is to extend the best educational opportunities possible to all children. Children from low-income families are particularly at risk because they currently receive inferior educations compared with more affluent children.

Employment projections for the year 2000 show a growth in the jobs requiring at least one year of college and a decline in those requiring a high school degree (Kutscher 1987). It is predicted that only 4 percent of jobs will hire employees with less than 9th grade education, 10 percent of jobs will require some high school, and 35 percent of jobs will hire high school graduates (Hudson Institute 1987). The remaining 52 percent of jobs will require at least some college education. Never before in history have over one-half of employees had to be educated beyond high school. Consequently, people without at least some college education will face increasing risks of being underemployed and unemployed. The first part of this chapter exposes the inequality of educational funding for schools in low-income districts and evaluates the effects unequal education has in the job market. Neither current funding nor current programs are sufficient enough to avoid a national labor and homelessness tragedy as we approach the year 2000. The second part of this chapter outlines suggestions for reforming the U.S. education system to better prepare it to meet the challenges that lie ahead.

The authors wish to express their appreciation to Michael Campbell, social worker for Caroline County Mental Health, Denton, Maryland, for discussions related to the suggestions made in this chapter.

Education and Resource Allocation

One way to find the real priorities of an organization is to evaluate fiscal policies and budget decisions. Although politicians and their constituents have given lip service to the importance of educating our youth, allocation of federal resources is restricted. Funding is largely left in the hands of local school districts. In 1987, the Department of Education was allocated 1.7 percent of the federal budget—$17.2 billion out of a $1,016.8 billion budget (Collender 1988). Federal money allocated to education pales when compared with the Department of Defense ($295.1 billion—29 percent of the federal budget). Educational priorities are questionable when the Funds Appropriated to the President ($12.1 billion) are 70 percent of the entire federal funds made available for education. Further, departments such as the Department of Transportation and the Department of Veterans Administration receive greater appropriations ($26 billion and $27 billion, respectively) than the Department of Education. To make matters worse, the proposed budget for 1988 allocated 15 percent less for education than 1987 ($14.7 billion).

Although not widely publicized with the rhetoric politicians use for education, transportation became a fiscal priority for the country as highways and other transportation facilities were built, allowing workers (particularly many professionals) to live in the suburbs and to commute to urban areas. Now a trend is developing to improve highway systems so that professionals can live in outlying country and rural areas and commute to urban areas. For example, the once small-town flare of two Maryland towns (Frederick and Westminster) are quickly becoming "bedroom communities," populated by professional employees of Washington, D.C. and Baltimore.

Another example of political priority matching with fiscal priority came when the United States bolstered services to veterans, resulting in the G.I. Bill and other veterans' benefits. Although funding for such veterans' programs is noteworthy and should continue to have priority, so too should the education of youth. If education is to be a true priority, substantial increase in federal money is needed.

Educating the Poor

Primary and Secondary Levels

Several alarming trends are jeopardizing the education of poor children. The hardest hit by cuts in education have been federal programs for poor elementary school children (cuts of $4.7 billion since 1982) [American Federation of State, County and Municipal Employees (AFSCME) 1988]. As we will explain in further detail later, early intervention is critical to establish a pattern of competence and success of children from low-income families. To curtail programs and services that can be instrumental in assisting children to maximize their potential as future wage earners is illogical and reprehensible. Further, "[with] numerous studies demonstrating that public investment in early and intensive help for educationally-disadvantaged children is repaid several times over in savings in remedial education, social welfare, corrections, and other costs, [the budget cuts] are also particularly short-sighted" (AFSCME 1988, p. 9).

In response to the 1983 *A Nation at Risk* report, state and local educational spending has increased, while federal spending has decreased (AFSCME 1988). Even though the report was a result of a major study commission appointed by President Reagan, the results were ignored in the creation of the federal budget. One can question the possibility of a hidden agenda by federal administrators to use this study commission to reduce federal involvement and increase the responsibility of state and local governments to resolve the educational crisis. Particularly suspicious is the fact that government spending decreased by approximately the same amounts state spending increased. The federal contribution to elementary and secondary education was 9.2 percent of the total school dollar in 1979–80, dropping to 6.7 percent in 1986–87 [Children's Defense Fund (CDF) 1989]. Among the problems created by such a shift is that no real increase occurred in money available for education. Additionally, because state and local governments avoided funding programs for poor and minority children, these children receive less assistance than before (CDF 1989). It is not surprising to discover that black youth are relatively worse off now than they were in the 1960s in rates of employment, delinquency, substance abuse, teenage pregnancy, and suicide (Gibbs 1984). And finally, children receive no federal protection against unequal resources between school districts within the nation. Spending in some school districts can be over twice as much per pupil than spending in other school districts within the same state. For example, in New Jersey (1986–87) spending ranged from $3,540 per student in one poor district to $7,642 per student in one wealthy district (CDF 1989). Such disparity in resource allocation is appalling in a nation predicated on equal opportunity, equal treatment, and mercy to those who are oppressed.

We believe it is no coincidence that during this time of federal cutbacks the plight of poor children in education has become worse. Consider the following information presented in *A Vision for America's Future:*

> Poor teens fall behind their peers: among 16-year-olds who have lived at least half of their lives in poverty, four out of 10 have repeated at least one grade—twice the repetition rate for 16-year-olds whose families have never lived in poverty. . . . Because they are more likely to suffer early disadvantages, black youths 15- to 17-years-old are more than twice as likely as white youths to have repeated a grade. Hispanic youths, often hampered by both poverty and language barriers, are almost three times as likely to have repeated a grade.

Poverty often spells poor skills: poor teenagers are four times more likely than nonpoor teens to have below-average basic academic skills. According to data from the National Longitudinal Survey of Young Americans, more than half of the 15- to 18-year-olds from families with incomes below poverty had reading and math skills that placed them in the bottom 20 percent of all teens. The data on minority teens, who bear a disproportionate burden of poverty, reflect these disadvantages. Although black and Hispanic students have made gains in reading achievement, the average reading level of minority 17-year-olds is only slightly better than the average reading level of white 13-year-olds.

Poor teens are more likely to drop out: despite overall improvement in the drop out rate, a distressingly large proportion of disadvantaged young people still leave school before graduation. Regardless of race, poor youths are almost three times more likely than their more well-off peers to drop out. In 1986 more than one in four poor 18- to 21-year-olds had dropped out of high school, compared with only one in 10 of their nonpoor peers. In large part because young black students face high poverty rates, a troubling gap in educational attainment between blacks and whites remains—though it has closed substantially over the past two decades and may narrow further as we approach the year 2000. (CDF 1989, pp. 69–70)

In addition to insufficient funding of low-income area schools, other factors implicit in a life of poverty help to explain why poor children are at high risk for school failure. First, as CDF (1989) explains, low-income people have little money to spend on medical care and nutritional food. For example, poor parents cannot afford the types of prenatal care that can increase the likelihood of normal development and birthweight, and after birth, poor children often receive inadequate nutrition by eating high-carbohydrate diets. Not often mentioned in this matter is that a culture of poverty exists, passed down from generation to generation, that can also affect utilization of services. For example, if parents grow up in a family where doctors were seen only in extreme cases, after home remedies failed, it would be difficult for some of these parents to begin a program of prenatal, and later, well-baby visits for their children, even if the visits and necessary transportation were at minimal or no cost.

Second, tough environmental conditions can impede a sense of trust and security needed for normal development. The net effect is that these children lag behind developmentally when compared with their more well-off counterparts, and they are predisposed for academic and behavioral problems. The CDF report indicates that children in poor communities get fewer opportunities for growth in the home and community environment. They emphasize the need for school, home, and community to work in a coordinated fashion to create a positive climate for children in which one setting reinforces the learning in other settings. However, not only do poor children have weak learning experiences in school, they also are faced with weak and negative social experiences in their homes and communities. Further, "[p]oor youths are more likely to have parents who have not completed high school than their non-poor peers. This is a significant disadvantage: parents' education level is one of the strongest predictors of their children's success in school" (CDF 1989, p. 74).

Third, poor children are more likely than children who are not poor to attend schools with inferior resources, often located in impoverished and sometimes dangerous localities. Despite the need for "the highest quality teachers, the most advanced classroom equipment, a low student/teacher ratio, and educational programs that supplement classroom learning" and the safest environment possible to overcome the deficits created by poverty, these children often receive substantially less than students who are not impoverished (CDF 1989, p. 73). Much of the disparity is caused by the differences in economic levels of school districts and the varying tax bases from which they must operate.

It is not a question of the abilities of educators and community representatives to handle and resolve the problem, but rather a question of loosening the fiscal restraints placed on educational and community systems. "There has never been a time in the life of the American public school when we have not known all we needed to in order to teach all those whom we chose to teach" (Edmonds 1979, p. 16). Failure of society to take full corrective action amounts to a choice to *not* adequately teach poor children.

The College Level

Federal cutbacks in education have also affected the ability of the poor to gain a college education. In the last decade, money available for college has substantially decreased, while college tuitions have substantially increased. Programs to assist students in managing college tuitions have been cut by $3.3 billion (AFSCME 1988). Again, the hardest hit by these cuts are the economically disadvantaged. Little difference existed in 1975 between poor and nonpoor high school graduates in obtaining at least one year of college (33.8 percent and 33.6 percent, respectively); however, in 1986 there was a 9-point gap between poor (29.9 percent) and nonpoor (38.5 percent) (CDF 1989). Children who grow up in poverty will be less likely than before to obtain the education needed to rise out of poverty.

Recommendations for Improving Education of the Poor

Equalization

The injustice of unequal funding between school districts can no longer be tolerated. The Supreme Court of Kentucky has taken an unprecedented step by ruling that the state educational system was unequal and therefore invalid and needed to be "re-created and re-established" (Walker 1989). No doubt such issues will eventually be addressed by the United States Supreme Court, yet years may pass in the interim. Therefore, to ensure equality in funding unilaterally across states, federal legislation is needed.

Proposals could involve plans of revenue sharing between school districts so that all schools receive equal appropriations. However, this would not necessarily eliminate the problem of disparity between states. Resolving the problem between states will probably require each school district in the nation to contribute a percentage of their revenue to a common fund that would be used in states that fall below the nationally set level for educational costs (after cost-of-living adjustments). Alternatively, the federal government could assume the responsibility of funding all public education through expanding the federal tax base and reducing state and local taxes.

Equalizing education in the United States, while a great asset in eliminating hidden discrimination to the poor and minorities, is not without great cost. Wealthy neighborhoods will notice a decline in their available educational funding, reducing their ability to receive preferential treatment for their children. However, if the federal government increases their monetary involvement, the decline will be less detrimental. Other indirect consequences will be felt by certain affluent communities, such as the decline in housing values caused by the leveling of disparity between school districts. In other words, the added advantage of a favorable school district to raise property value will be removed, since schools will be more equal in their quality and services.

Federal Involvement

A national equalization program would require supervision from a federal department, such as the Department of Education. Although a national plan would help to put school districts on equal footing for the first fiscal year of its operation, previously underfunded schools will be striving to rebuild after years of neglect. These schools should be entitled to special federal equalization grants appropriated to school districts by need.

The state and local governments will not be able to bear the full cost of education, and consequently the federal government needs to increase its percentage of education funding. In addition, the federal government should increase funding to programs that assist disadvantaged children. For example, a federal program entitled "Chapter 1" offers remedial education to poor children who are at risk of falling behind in school. Despite the fact that Chapter 1 has resulted in significant academic gains of needy children, its funding only allowed it to serve 54 of 100 poor children in 1985, compared with 75 of 100 in 1980 (CDF 1989). Federal funding should make it possible for such a program to serve all children in need.

If funds are increased to serve poor students, there should also be accountability and assurance that appropriations are being utilized effectively. The educational system has to be held accountable for sound planning and management of funded programs. The embarrassment of the Washington, D.C. school system is an example of how funding was available but not well-managed. "School officials hastily arranged [a] summer program [in the spring of 1989], after being embarrassed by the discovery that a $400,000 dropout prevention grant from the U.S. Department of Education had hardly been touched" (Sanchez 1989, p. B1). Even though early reports of the summer program (a portion of the grant) were positive, members of the legislative and executive branches of government, as well as taxpayers, are left feeling uneasy and apprehensive about future appropriations.

Federal grants should be made available to explore and discover other effective programs. Increasing funding for demonstration grants (grants that fund the operation and evaluation of experimental programs) and direct research grants will make new options possible.

As we move into the 1990s, quality education for children is an often-voiced concern of parents and the nation, yet a low-budget mentality is still evident. In part, the future of this country is dependent on the success of the educational system. A report of business leaders (Committee for Economic Development 1987) concluded that the U.S. economy will not be able to grow because the "educational underclass" will be unable to meet the demands of jobs that require increased skills. They believe that if the problem continues the result will impoverish the nation because we will no longer be competitive in world trade. Increasing funds for education is not only the most humane course of action, it is also a wise and necessary investment.

Paving the Way to College

Given the fact that the economy is quickly moving into a period in which a college degree, instead of a high school degree, will be the minimum required to obtain well-paying employment, it is particularly important to examine policy options for resolving this crisis. With the rise in college tuition costs, it is more important than ever to assist poorer students in financing their education.

Obviously, efforts must be directed at both a means of financing college education and some process by which college tuition costs can be controlled. Two frequently discussed approaches to address financing college education are to increase grant support and for the federal government to loan students money to pay for their tuition and then tax the student's income upon graduation until the tuition is repaid.

Another concern is the sharply rising cost of college tuition. Currently, there is no national oversight of these costs, and while there may be justifiable reasons for the sharp increases, some oversight is still warranted.

Assuming that these matters can be resolved, it is of vital importance to examine current educational policies that purposely discourage some children from going to college. For example, most children who lack motivation, are uninterested, are underachievers, or are management problems are channeled into non-college-oriented courses. While in the short run this may benefit the child, as adults, they may find themselves only able to work in low-paying jobs. Unlike in the past when the manufacturing sector offered many individuals the opportunity to make relatively high wages without high levels of education, the job market is increasingly discriminating against those without college educations. Clearly a new approach is needed that emphasizes encouraging rather than discouraging children to consider college.

Building Competence Through Specialized Planning

One major goal of education is to help children to experience themselves as competent and successful. Making the most of raw talents and intellectual abilities requires competence that breeds hope and motivation. Making the most of one's talents leads to success, which becomes the impetus for further success, creating an upward spiral of advancement. Alternatively, lack of competence, motivation, and confidence can lead to below-potential efforts and failure, which further fuels low competence and motivation levels. Along with complications in achievement, this type of spiraling can increase hopelessness, unworthiness, shame, depression, and anger, which may lead to behavioral problems as an additional complication. Learning can become an unpleasant experience. Longitudinal information on 5th and 6th graders shows that without intervention, self-concepts of low-income youth remain relatively the same through high school (Barnes & Farrier 1985).

Building competence in children requires more than making it an aspect within a philosophy of education; instead, it demands specific planning and allocation of resources. For example, a program should be created in all schools that identifies underachieving children and establishes an individualized plan that capitalizes on strengths and builds up areas of deficit. The plan is designed to break down goals into attainable steps, allowing children to experience success. Time periods are set for evaluation, and if underachieving is still evident, the school system is held responsible for providing the professional intervention needed to get children on track.

Particularly problematic are children who disrupt classrooms and who jeopardize the safety of students and faculty. These "acting-out" students could be treated as they were by Joe Clark, a principal in New Jersey, who threatened them with a baseball bat and expulsion. This approach labeled as "troublesome" those students whom the schools had failed to challenge, and removed them from the educational system. While studies have shown this approach may reduce violence in the schools, it is doubtful that the community will benefit (Toby 1983). Instead, these individuals will join the ranks of the long-term unemployed and become vulnerable to homelessness.

An alternative approach is to seek methods of prevention that will challenge students, both troublesome and untroubled, to remain in school. Obviously, the student's vision of the future is key to making the challenge more than window dressing. For these children in the urban underclass and for others who grow up in poverty, the vision of the future has been shaped by disappointment, failure, and economic deprivation. Their hopelessness, which is frequently manifested in frustration and rage, is in many ways a reflection of their negative life experiences.

Lowering Teacher/Student Ratios

In the often crowded and stressed atmosphere of schools in poor districts, the one-to-one interaction between student and teacher is reduced. However, the relationship between student and teacher often plays a significant role in how children view themselves and their potential. Also, children, because they are easily embarrassed and intimated, often do not seek the help they need in larger groups. One underachieving student reported: "A lot of times you get frustrated when you don't understand what the teacher is talking about. But you don't want to ask her because kids might laugh. You can see kids wanting to ask so bad, but they just don't" (Sanchez 1989, p. B7).

A highly desirable factor in any program to assist underachieving students is a close personal investment of supportive teachers in the learning of students. Schools in poor districts should create teacher/student ratios that allow this type of quality relationship.

Programs that have provided children with more attention in small settings are demonstrating success. For example, one successful program in New York City divided the students into "houses" of 75 students. Each house had its own faculty, and classes were kept at 18 students or less (CDF 1989).

Summer Programs

For many urban poor children, the summer is a time for playing in the streets and in vacant lots covered with broken glass. City property is often poorly kept and riddled with graffiti and other vandalism. The streets offer drugs, sex and violence, and temptation for deviant behavior. Although an investment into summer programs will provide a meaningful experience with life-long dividends for children and reduce crime and vandalism, summer programs are not well-funded.

Summer camps provide an excellent setting for bolstering academic and social skills and for providing an environment for prosocial modeling and building competence. In addition, camps provide an appropriate setting for developing a normative climate against drugs, violence, and premarital sex. Skills and other gains made in a camping program can be reinforced and maintained through community-based programs and school programs throughout the year. The cost of residential camping is only a fraction of the expense of institutional placement or grade repetitions.

The few camps that provide service to poor children are in jeopardy. For example, low-income children from Baltimore have been invited to a free residential camping experience for the past sixty years, sponsored by the St. Vincent de Paul Society. The camp, currently located off the South River in Annapolis, is open to children of all faiths and race. However, yearly deficit spending threatens to close this much-needed program. One of the authors is personally familiar with the benefits of this camp program because he was a camper at this camp many years ago.

The authors are currently developing ideas for a residential camp program that will be designed to accomplish the following goals: a) to provide a setting where academic skills can be promoted in a caring and supportive environment; b) to include education concerning the economy and work-related roles; c) to provide a normative climate against drugs and premarital sex; d) to provide positive role models; e) to bolster self-esteem, contentment, and a sense of competence; f) to offer fun recreational activities; g) to establish follow-up programs in communities and schools; and h) to set up a research design to evaluate the effectiveness of such a program.

Another summer alternative is to create day programs using the school buildings and resources. These programs can focus on the combination of learning and recreation similar to that suggested above. The highlight of such programs would be the supportive environment created by low teacher/student ratios, emphasis on education as enjoyable, competence building, and the reinforcement of summer recreation. The Washington, D.C. program conducted in the summer of 1989, despite its hasty planning, illustrates the effective use of such a combination. In the morning, students focused on academic subjects and special workshop presentations under close supervision of supportive adults, and in the afternoon, special trips and recreational activities were planned.

After-School Programs

Traditionally, staying after school meant that something went wrong during the day. However, in the case of after-school programs, staying after school can lead to meaningful learning experiences. Such programs can offer children one-to-one attention that not only increases learning, but reinforces positive self-worth.

Several direct and indirect benefits are gained from after-school programs: first, they can be the setting for special programs targeted for improving the lives of poor children; second, they can provide tutoring and special help with homework; third, recreational and other enrichment activities can be used to reinforce learning and provide productive outlets for children; fourth, early creation of proper study habits can have a lifelong impact on benefits gained from educational opportunities; fifth, parents can be hired to assist in these programs, which increases the adult/child ratio and creates opportunities for additional income for families; and finally, sixth, parents benefit from the after-school care that allows them to continue full-time employment.

Building Incentives for Quality Educators

The mindset of spending little for education is not altogether baffling from a historical view of education. In the years prior to the 1900s, when children were old enough to carry full-time work responsibilities (usually around twelve years of age), they either helped on the family farm or ranch or became apprentices for certain trades. School was not seen as completely necessary, but often it was tolerated for children below the age of twelve.

Three factors in particular kept salaries for teachers low: a) the occupation of teaching was not seen as productive for preparing students for the work force; b) it was valued less because it was a service for children in an adult-oriented society; and c) many early teachers were religious clergy who taught children at low or no cost, which created a mindset of low-budget education. Because teaching did not pay a wage to support a family, many men avoided becoming teachers. Taken together with the discrimination of women in the work force, teaching salaries continue to be low. In many states teachers are currently paid less than sanitation workers and janitors.

In recent decades, education has become the primary way we prepare youth for employment. Although there has been a dramatic shift in the association between education and employment, pay for teachers has increased at only incremental levels. Teachers are forced to leave education because they cannot afford to live and raise their children as desired on their salaries. When possible, many teachers avoid taking positions in poor districts because of reduced pay, poor benefits, inferior resources, tougher child management problems, and fears for their physical safety. Building incentives through financial compensation and job benefits can help to attract quality teachers and administrators to poor areas.

Empowering Parents

It is difficult to determine the role parental influence can have on drop-out decisions of children. One study found lack of parental support and employment problems to be predictors of depression and a negative view of self

(Simons & Miller 1987). We assume that these negative conditions are relevant to drop-out decisions. Some parents do not offer positive support to assist their children in the struggle of staying in school. However, some children will do poorly in school, and may drop out, regardless of positive efforts made by parents.

Educating parents to start early in supporting and training their children to become academically successful is important. Emphasis should be on coordinating an academic plan that involves school and home. For example, schools can coordinate with parents a system of reinforcement that parents provide in the home for academic success at school (for a program example see DiBlasio 1989a). Viewing parents as valuable team members in the educational system and actively reaching out to them is critical. Incentives for parental participation can be built into school programs. For example, families that are involved in special school programs might receive discounts on services, goods, and entertainment from local merchants (arranged by school counselors or social workers). Creating incentives within the tax structure for participating families would also be helpful.

Designing Curricula and Programs Relevant to Economic Well-Being

A missing ingredient in many educational programs is a coordinated plan that connects academic skills with skills that will help students survive in the economy. Children from middle-class families are readily exposed to such concepts as budgeting, investment, comparative shopping, savings, interest, checking accounts, and job-related skills and values. These and other important economic concepts could be easily integrated in existing academic subjects such as math and social studies. A well-planned and joint effort of educators and business people could produce a meaningful program for kindergarten through 12th grade.

Examples of types of learning experiences and activities include: following a particular stock through the newspaper throughout the school year; using advertisements to find the best price on major items; inventing economies in which each child is responsible for managing pretend money (i.e., paying bills, savings, investment, etc.); field trips to banking institutions; and budget creation and effective use of money. In regard to job-related skills and values, examples include: steps in successful interviewing; responsible work behavior, such as promptness, neatness, dependability; field trips to various work settings; and career days when professionals and craftsmen are invited to talk about their occupations.

Updating technology in the school systems is important in an age when technological advances are occurring at rapid rates. Keeping the curricula relevant requires technology that keeps pace with that found in the marketplace. Most relevant technological advances in business and science require the utilization of current computer systems and software packages. The sharing of computer facilities and technology between state universities and public school systems could open the door for advance training opportunities. For example, mainframe access and supportive services could be made available to high schools. Federal funding and legislation mandating the sharing of resources would be required to equalize opportunities between states.

Early Detection and Prevention

The regular school system has failed to engage many young children before academic, attitudinal, and behavioral problems have developed to almost irreversible proportions. Some measure of the potential for completing school should be required of all students at elementary levels. Children who demonstrate drop-out potential should receive special preventive services. For example, poverty is one factor in drop-out potential: poor children are three times more likely than others to drop out of school (CDF 1989).

Poverty and other life stresses, such as family dysfunction, violence in the community, and drugs, can produce emotional problems for some students that block learning and success. For example, children tend to act out behaviorally and become hyperactive when they are depressed (Carlson & Cantwell 1970). Associated with depression is low self-esteem, which in turn accentuates depression, thereby increasing acting-out behaviors (Kaslow et al. 1984). Adults often respond to this acting out with frustration, anger, and punishment, aggravating the depression and sending messages attacking self-worth. It is no wonder these children fail to learn and are simply passed along until they are old enough to drop out. Many of these children find acceptance in deviant groups that support acting out and drug use.

Application of measures such as the Hudson Clinical Measurement Package (1982) provide a reliable and easily scored measure of a variety of psychosocial variables. Measures include the Generalized Contentment Scale (a measure of depression); the Index of Self-Esteem; the Index of Peer Relations; the Index of Family Relations; the Child's Attitude Toward Mother; The Child's Attitude Toward Father; the Index of Parental Attitudes; and the Clinical Anxiety Scale. Scoring indicates when there is a need for professional intervention. In addition, Conner's Hyperactivity Scales (1970) (rated by parents and teachers) are helpful in determining levels of hyperactive behavior. Increased funding for school psychologists and social workers to do preventive work is necessary if early detection is to be fruitful.

Learning disabilities are also problematic and add to the drop-out equation. Learning disabilities are often undetected, and during elementary school years children label themselves (and are often labeled) "dumb" and "slow." This contributes to low self-regard, lack of motivation, and learned helplessness (Seligman 1975). One of the authors taught a graduate student who, despite her alertness and participation in class, did poorly on written examinations. The student knew she had problems throughout her life with examinations, but was convinced by school counselors that she suffered from test anxiety. She described herself as intellectually slow, but was determined to work many times harder than her classmates to make it through. The author referred her for learning disability testing, and it was discovered that she had an 8th grade reading level due to a significant learning disability. Many children would have (and do) quit before graduating from high school, but despite the odds, she completed not only high school, but also college and graduate school. Her fortitude and strength of determination is rare.

All children who demonstrate low performance in academic subjects or behavior should receive periodic screening for learning disabilities. In addition, physical and mental health disorders such as poor hearing and eyesight, organic brain dysfunction, hyper- and hypo-thyroidism, hypoglycemia, dysthymia, major depression, attention deficit, and hyperactivity disorder must be evaluated. (See American Psychiatric Association, 1987, for a list of mental health disorders.)

Early detection and prevention of learning disabilities and other problems is made possible by programs such as Head Start. This program has received federal funding since the 1960s and provides educational and concrete services to very young children (3- and 4-year olds) and parents of low-income families. Even though Head Start has demonstrated profound success, its funding has not kept pace with need. Currently, it can only serve one out of the six children who are eligible, compared with one in four in 1978 (CDF 1989). Why design programs that are effective and provide them funding for only 17 percent of the job? Again, the funding is particularly short-sighted, given that every dollar invested in Head Start saves six dollars in special education, grade retention, public assistance, and crime (CDF 1989).

Other programs implemented in kindergarten and 1st grade also have been clearly successful (Sparrow et al. 1983). One study implemented in two elementary schools provided a representative governance group, a parent-participation program and group, a mental health program and team, and an academic program and found that participants had increased academic and social gains when compared with the control group (Comer 1985). These programs should receive full funding, and the Head Start program should be extended to serve all preschool children (infants through 5-year-olds).

Community Involvement Through Sponsorship Programs

Traditionally, causes that advocated the betterment of children have attracted volunteers and financial support from community businesses and other organizations. We suggest sponsorship programs in which specific schools in low-income areas are "adopted" by community businesses and organizations. These schools would then receive a number of services and financial assistance from these organizations, such as updated equipment, guest lectures, job-skill training, interview training, and use of business resources.

Children in these sponsored schools would receive first-hand information about various professions and trades. Role modeling opportunities would also result when children are exposed to the direct involvement of local community professionals. This exposure may assist children in new visions for their future. For older students, companies can establish summer work programs and also provide schools with a number of full-time jobs it will commit to their graduates.

In addition to school adoption, businesses could adopt certain at-risk children and provide them with financial and educational opportunities from elementary school through their college years. Such individual sponsorships could end with a guaranteed job interview with the company after completion of educational training.

Universities and colleges are in an excellent position to provide tremendous educational experiences and resources to poor school districts. For example, the University of Maryland at Baltimore took on the challenge of supporting a local school. The University provided high quality instruction, shared resources (such as computer facilities), and met many health and dental needs of the students. The exposure of students to faculty and staff of the dental, legal, medical, nursing, pharmacy, and social work graduate schools introduced them to a variety of professional roles.

Building Resistance to Drugs and Premarital Sex

Drugs, teenage pregnancy, and violence have reached all-time highs in this country. The effects of the AIDS virus on the teenage population has yet to be determined. Students in low-income school districts are particularly vulnerable to these problems. Not only are drugs prevalent on the streets, but also in many low-income neighborhoods it is considered routine for young males to father children and young females to become mothers prior to adulthood. For example, when asked to project themselves into future roles, the tendency of female adolescents from low socioeconomic status was to see themselves becoming mothers in the near future, instead of roles such as career women or even spouses (Shtarkshall 1987). Findings solutions to these problems has been extremely difficult. Nonetheless, educators, parents, and others must continue in full-scale and comprehensive ways to reduce the incidence of teenage sexual promiscuity.

Whereas the federal and state governments have provided funding for demonstration projects and research grants, their ongoing funding for prevention programs must increase. In addition, funding for programs that have not clearly demonstrated significant success must be redirected. Such is the case of sixteen years' worth of failed efforts of school-based clinics to reduce the incidence of teenage pregnancies through counseling and dissemination of free birth control to students (see Harold 1988 and DiBlasio 1988a for a point/counterpoint discussion of school-based clinics).

A rather well-developed literature is available concerning adolescent drinking, drug use, and other deviant behavior. This literature largely suggests that deviant behavior is contributed to through emulation of parent models and peer reinforcement and association (Akers et al. 1979; Bandura 1969; Alexander & Campbell 1967; DiBlasio 1986, 1987, 1988b; Coombs & Dickenson 1981; Jessor & Jessor 1977). Less is known about the sexual behavior of adolescents primarily because the research has focused on age of onset, prevalence and incidence, and demographical categories (Hayes 1987; Jorgensen 1983).

Combining differential association theory (Sutherland & Cressey 1978) and social learning theory (Bandura 1969; Skinner 1953) has demonstrated explanatory power for adolescent drinking and drug use (Akers et al. 1979), adolescent drinking and driving (DiBlasio 1986), adolescents riding with drinking drivers (DiBlasio 1988), and adolescent sex (DiBlasio & Benda, in press).

The following is a brief explanation of the theory:

> Social behavior is understood through studying the impact of differential association with adults and peers, internalization of group norms (normative definitions), modeling, and the interaction of positive and negative reinforcement (differential reinforcement).
>
> Individuals learn behaviors in social groups, such as family and peer-friendship groups. If the association is intense, is frequent, and holds certain priority, individuals will tend to learn and act in ways consistent with the behavioral patterns of the group (Sutherland 1947). Differential association is the exposure and identification to various groups. Groups influence the development of the normative definitions of each member. Normative definitions are personal attitudes and beliefs about rules, laws, and values. These personal attitudes and beliefs help guide the individual in making choices to act in law-abiding or law-violating ways.
>
> Modeling and differential reinforcement also occur within the context of significant groups. The behaviors of adults and peers are observed (or perceived to have occurred) and imitated by adolescents. The frequency of participation in the learned behaviors is partly contingent on the negative and positive reinforcement received. A person will want to increase positive reinforcement and decrease negative consequences. Differential reinforcement is the balance of positive reinforcement and reward (benefit) measured against the negative reinforcement (cost) of both the behavior . . . and the alternative behavior. . . . The adolescent will tend to participate in the behavior that provides the most perceived and actual benefits when compared to the perceived or actual costs. (Di Blasio 1986, p. 175)

Comprehensive prevention strategies should account for the primary variables described above (differential association, normative definitions, differential reinforcement, and modeling). For example, instead of excluding peers who frequently are engaged in deviant behavior, they should be invited to participate in planning prevention strategies. Providing adolescents with central responsibilities increases the likelihood that peer reinforcement will work in prosocial ways (for an example see DiBlasio 1987). Creating a system of peer counselors and investing them with certain responsibilities and privileges is another way to involve all types of adolescents. Programs that promote resistance, such as the "say no" campaigns, hold particular value, since they use peer involvement, supply positive reinforcement, establish prosocial normative climates, and use adult and peer modeling. In addition, helping professionals must continue to ask themselves how their values and beliefs influence children and adolescents (DiBlasio 1989).

This discussion only touches the surface of a very complicated issue needing resolution. Ultimately, schools must design programs that will decrease acting-out behaviors that interfere with the learning process that often lead to failure and dropping out.

In Summary

The crisis of homelessness will escalate to intolerable levels if predicted trends continue in educational requirements needed for employment. Major reform is needed in education to prepare youth for the reality of the future job market. Not providing quality and equal education to children, particularly to children in poor school districts, is a serious form of oppression that has lifelong debilitating effects for children and for the United States. If we are to be successful in prevention, immediate action along the lines suggested in this chapter is necessary.

The next chapter presents another crisis associated with homelessness: the rising costs and unavailability of housing.

References

Akers, R.C., Krohn, M.D., Lanza-Koduce, L. & Radosevich, M. (1979). Social learning and deviant behavior: A specific test to general theory. *American Sociological Review, 44,* 636–55.

Alexander, N.C. & Campbell, E.Q. (1967). Peer influences on alcohol drinking. *Quarterly Journal of Studies on Alcohol, 28,* 444–53.

American Federation of State, County, and Municipal Employees (AFSCME) (1988). *The Republican record: A 7-year analysis of state losses of federal funding FY 1982–FY 1988).* Washington, D.C.: AFSCME.

American Psychiatric Association (APA) (1987). *Diagnostic and statistical manual,* 3rd Ed., revised. Washington, D.C.: APA.

Bandura, A. (1969). *Principles of behavior modification.* New York: Holt, Rinehart & Winston.

Barnes, M.E. & Farrier, S.C. (1985). A longitudinal study of the self-concept of low-income youth. *Adolescence, 20,* 199–205.

Carlson, G. & Cantwell, D. (1970). Unmasking masked depression in children and adolescents. *American Journal of Psychiatry, 137,* 445–49.

Children's Defense Fund (CDF) (1989). *A Vision for America's Future.* Washington, D.C.: CDF.

Collender, S.E. (1988). *The Guide to the Federal Budget.* Washington, D.C.: The Urban Institute Press.

Comer, J.P. (1985). The Yale–New Haven Primary Prevention Project: A follow-up study. *Journal of the American Academy of Child Psychiatry, 24,* 154–60.

Committee for Economic Development (1987). Children in need: Investment strategies for the educationally disadvantaged, cited in CDF, *A Vision for America's Future.* Washington, D.C.

Conners, C.K. (1970). Symptom patterns in hyperkinetic, neurotic and normal children. *Child Development, 41,* 667–82.

Coombs, R.H. & Dickenson, K.M. (1981). Generational continuity in the use of alcohol and other substances: A literature review. *Abstracts Review on Alcohol and Driving, 2,* (4): 1–7.

DiBlasio, F.A. (1986). Drinking adolescents on the roads. *Journal of Youth and Adolescence, 15,* 173–88.

———. (1987). Social learning variables in preventing adolescent drinking and driving: Implications for school social workers. *School Social Work Journal, 12,* 18–25.

———. (1988a). A time to question school-based clinics. *Health and Social Work, 13,* 305–07.

———. (1988b). Predriving riders and drinking drivers. *Journal of Studies on Alcohol, 49,* 11–15.

———. (1989a). Behavioral program for hyperactive students. *Social Work in Education, 12,* 45–52.

———. (1989b). Adolescent sexuality: Promoting the search for hidden values. *Child Welfare, 68,* 331–37.

DiBlasio, F.A. & Benda, B. (In press). Adolescent sexual behavior: Multivariate analysis of a social learning model. *Journal of Adolescent Research.*

Edmonds, R. (1979). Effective schools for the urban poor. *Education Leadership, 37,* 15–24.

Gibbs, J.T. (1984). Black adolescents and youth: An endangered species. *American Journal of Orthopsychiatry, 54,* 6–21.

Harold, N.B. (1988). School-based clinics effectively meet needs of adolescents. *Health and Social Work, 13,* 305–7.

Hayes, C.D. (ed.) (1987). *Risking the Future: Adolescent Sexuality, Pregnancy and Childbearing.* Washington, D.C: National Academy Press.

Hudson Institute, Inc. (1987). *Workforce 2000: Work and Workers for the 21st Century.* Washington, D.C.: U.S. Department of Labor.

Hudson, W.W. (1982). *The Clinical Measurement Package.* Chicago: Dorsey Press.

Jessor, R. & Jessor, S.L. (1977). *Problem Behavior and Psychosocial Development: A Longitudinal Study of Youth.* New York: Academic Press.

Jorgensen, S.R. (1983). Beyond adolescent pregnancy: Research frontiers for early adolescent sexuality. *Journal of Early Adolescence, 3,* 141–55.

Kaslow, N.J., Rehm, L.P. & Siegel, A.W. (1984). Social-cognitive and cognitive correlates of depression in children. *Journal of Abnormal Child Psychology, 12,* 605–20.

Kutscher, R.E. (1987). Overview and implications of the projections to 2000. *Monthly Labor Review, 110, 5.*

Sanchez, R. (1989). D.C. students succeed at 2nd chance. Washington, D.C.: *Washington Post,* August 19, B1, B7.

Seligman, M.E. (1975). *Helplessness: On Depression, Development and Death.* San Francisco: W.H. Freeman & Co.

Shtarkshall, R.A. (1987). Motherhood as a dominant feature in the self-image of female adolescents of low socioeconomic status. *Adolescence, 22,* 565–70.

Simons, R.L. & Miller, M.G. (1987). Adolescent depression: Assessing the impact of negative cognitions and socioenvironmental problems. *Social Work, 32,* 326–29.

Skinner, B.F. (1953). *Science and Human Behavior.* New York: Macmillan.

Sparrow, S.S., Blachman, B.A. & Chauncey, S. (1983). Diagnostic and prescriptive intervention in primary school education. *American Journal of Orthopsychiatry, 53,* 721–29.

Sutherland, E.H. (1947). *Principles of Criminology,* 4th ed. Chicago: J.B. Lippincott.

Sutherland, E.H. & Cressey, D.R. (1978). *Principles of Criminology,* 10th ed. Chicago: J.B. Lippincott.

Toby, J. (1983). *Violence in schools: National Institute of Justice Brief.* Washington, D.C.: U.S. Department of Justice.

Walker, R. (1989). Entire Kentucky school system is ruled invalid. *Education Week, 8,* 1, 14.

5
Housing: A Commodity or a Right?

Historically, housing in the United States has been viewed as a commodity—something that is purchased, held for a time, and sold for
a profit. As opposed to Canada, where home mortgage interest is
not deductible, tax laws in United States direct a significant portion of savings
to housing. For example:

> [T]he total amount of federal subsidies (from both subsidized housing pro-
> grams and tax benefits) going to the higher income (those households with
> incomes over $50,000 a year) group is more than three times the amount
> going to the lower income group. (Center on Budget and Policy Priorities,
> 1989, p. XVII)

What policies are needed to enable more Americans to afford housing?
The answer to this question demands that we, as a society, resolve the question of whether housing is a privilege or a right. If it is a privilege, then
homelessness will have to be tolerated. Because some individuals and families
will simply be unable to afford to shelter themselves. On the other hand, if
housing is a right, then wealth needs to be redistributed in such a way that
access to housing is guaranteed for everyone.

We believe that housing is a right and subsidies are necessary; however,
the thrust of these initiatives should favor those individuals and families that
actually need assistance. As Kuttner (1984) observes:

> In reality, we don't over subsidize 'housing'; we over subsidize rich people's
> housing. From that point of view of a young family looking at $1000
> monthly payments as the ticket of admission to their first house, housing is
> not over subsidized at all. From the perspective of a millionaire con-
> templating whether to trade in a tax-sheltered $400,000 house for a tax-
> sheltered $600,000 capital gain, housing is nicely subsidized indeed. (p. 66)

Before discussing specific initiatives that would create greater housing opportunities for the young, poor, and near poor, it is important to review the combination of factors that have created a lack of affordable housing.

Trickle-Down Housing for the Poor

Thus far, the Stewart B. McKinney Homeless Assistance Act (H.R. 286, 1987) has been the major federal legislation developed to address the chronic housing shortage. The Bush budget has proposed funding for the project at $378 million for fiscal year 1989. At the same time, President Bush proposed eliminating 50 percent of the number of low-income households provided with housing aid through the rural programs of the Department of Agriculture. Underlying this legislation is the belief that the "rising tide" created by continued prosperity and affluence will pull the poor up from poverty.

Conservatives, in particular, argue that by developing more homes for the wealthy, a greater supply of housing for the poor also will be created (Weicher 1987). This is referred to as *filtering,* in which the cost of older and more modest houses fall as the former occupant buys more expensive housing (Quigley 1979). Filtering is more of an illusion than a reality. In fact, housing as an asset tends to appreciate. During the 1970s, for example, inflation increased the net worth of many homeowners.

Prior to the 1970s, there was agreement among many, both conservative and liberal, that it was appropriate for the federal government to intervene in housing issues. By the early 1970s, most middle-income Americans were comfortably housed, and it was primarily the poor who were confronted with inadequate housing. Why had middle-income Americans been able to adequately house themselves, yet many of the poor remain inadequately housed?

The roots of this phenomenon go back to the nineteenth century, when an emerging middle class began to generate savings that they invested in savings accounts and life insurance policies. Financial institutions turned to housing construction as one avenue to direct this new flow of capital. Stone (1980–81) points out that between 1900 and 1930, residential mortgage debt grew from less than $3 billion to over $30 billion. In fact, "mortgage debt grew in the 1920s four times faster than the overall economy" (Stone 1986, p. 50). The economy collapsed toward the end of the decade, and millions of people lost their homes through foreclosure. Banks were left with worthless pieces of real estate and were not able to pay off their savings depositors.

Efforts to rebuild the shattered economy led to the creation of the Reconstruction Finance Corporation, which enabled redevelopment housing corporations to rehabilitate slums (Scott 1971). Thrift institutions were created through the joint initiatives of the Homeowners Loan Act of 1933 and the National Housing Act of 1934. The goal of these intitiatives was to extend private credit, not public funds, to a greater number of Americans. Some scholars argue that court injunction and political backlash quickly eliminated or blunted the positive effects of these programs by not extending credit to a greater number of Americans (Sternlieb & Listokin 1987). However, other scholars (Stone 1986) argue that the main thrust of these programs was to stabilize the mortgage industry at the expense of making housing a right for every American.

Rising incomes of the 1940s, 1950s, and early 1960s enabled millions of Americans to buy homes in the rapidly developing suburbs. Federal housing policy, such as the Federal Housing Administration home mortgage insurance programs, benefited both middle-income buyers and developers when they chose to locate in the suburbs (Gelfand 1975). The rush to develop the suburbs was so great that federal programs sought developers willing to build suburban homes (Stone 1973). Meanwhile, federal housing policy neglected central cities with their growing concentrations of poverty-stricken minority populations. Once again, the thrust of federal housing policy favored the interests of capital at the expense of the poor.

By the late 1960s, residential mortgage debt was growing at a faster rate (about three times faster) than the Gross National Product (GNP) and disposable personal income (Stone 1986). This meant that the housing industry was increasingly dependent on credit, which was dependent on the prevailing interest rate. As long as the economy prospered, much like in the 1920s, Americans were able to shoulder the debt necessary to afford the "American dream"; however, the economic crisis of the 1970s and particularly the 1981 recession made many people realize that home ownership was no longer possible for all Americans.

In 1980, mortgage interest rates reached 16 to 17 percent. The median price of a new home rose 50 percent, prices for existing homes rose over 70 percent, and mortgage interest rates rose 9 percent. The ability of families to afford new homes graphically declined; in the 1950s, two-thirds of all families could afford a new home, by 1970, the proportion had declined to one-half, and by 1976, the proportion had declined to one-fourth. In 1985, the latest year for which comprehensive statistics on housing are available, 38 percent of poor home owners spent at least 50 percent of their incomes for housing expenses. Approximately 63 percent of low-income renters paid over 50 percent of their income for housing. On the other hand, a household with an income between $40,000 and $60,000 per year paid only 14 percent of their income for housing. In 1989, only 50 percent of married couples aged 25 to 35 qualified for an 80 percent mortgage (Schmid 1989).

Despite the creation of the Federal National Mortgage Association and the Federal Home Loan Mortgage Association, the country's increasing demand for mortgage debt has not been satisfied. These organizations are designed to create a broader market in which private funds could be attracted to thrifts and savings and loans. However, the ever-increasing debt has fueled higher interest rates, and efforts by the Federal Reserve to combat inflation have led to collapses in the housing market, especially between 1980 and 1982. Meanwhile, those consumers who have been able to obtain a mortgage are paying as much as 60 percent of their disposable income for housing, and mortgage delinquencies are at an all-time high (Belcher & Singer 1988).

Rents and the Poor

Instead of a rising tide in which people filter up to more expensive housing, the result of the increasing inability of many Americans to afford the "American dream" of home ownership results in a greater demand for rental units. As a result, the cost of renting has gone up dramatically. This process has particularly hurt the poor. Whereas rents have increased more slowly than the Consumer Price Index, they have risen faster than tenant incomes (Dolbeare 1983). By 1983, half of low-income families were paying over 72 percent of their incomes for rent (Dolbeare 1983). Estimates suggest that over the last decade, rents have risen nearly twice as fast as tenant incomes (Hopper & Hamberg 1986). In 1985,

> [s]ome 45 percent of all poor renter households—or 3.1 million poor households—paid at least 70 percent of their incomes for housing costs (i.e., rent and utilities). (Center on Budget and Policy Priorities, 1989, p. 1)

Contrary to conventional wisdom, rent prices are not determined by supply and demand. Instead, tenants are at a distinctly unfair disadvantage. In fact, numerous studies have concluded that the majority of the rental housing is controlled by a few owners (Appelbaum & Glasser 1982; Linson 1978; Gilderbloom & Keating 1982). These few owners are able to control and manipulate prices to their benefit. Tenants and those seeking rental units are less organized and more numerous. Owners, on the other hand, belong to organizations such as the National Association of Realtors that educate and encourage owners to raise rents. Absentee owners, such as professionals who purchase the properties for the tax write-off and income, frequently use management companies that charge an average of $168 "a year per unit more than it costs owners who manage their units themselves." (Gray 1979)

Owner-dominated organizations charge that land-use regulations and other artificial constraints, such as a requirement that developers use a certain grade of lumber, account for the rise in rents. Appelbaum and Gilderbloom (1986) argue that "no more than 15 percent of differences in price between areas" are accounted for by these artificial constraints. Reasons for this vary; the most obvious is that government controls often fail because corporations find a way to avoid them.

Unlike with other commodities such as oranges, consumers are very limited, and often unable, to substitute another commodity for rental units. Admittedly, some individuals and families are able to pay more for rent or to buy a home, but the poor are unable to do this. The poor, however, must pay whatever the landlords charge or become homeless. As owners find that they cannot raise rents because the poor are unable to pay higher rents, they convert their investments to condominiums (U.S. Congress, Congressional Budget Office 1981, pp. 32–36). This in turn reduces the supply of affordable housing stock for low-income families.

Conversion of apartments into condominiums is a natural, although negative outgrowth of the fact that real estate investments must compete against other investments within an owner's portfolio. The return on a rental unit is weighed against other potential investments. If, during a time of rising interest rates, the cost of operating the units becomes such that the rate of return drops, the owner is likely to try to raise the rent, and when that fails, sell the asset. This in turn leads to speculation as realtors create value by rapidly turning over land or housing. The notion of *created value* refers to a process whereby realtors use public relations and marketing strategies to inflate the price of land. It should be noted, however, that the land itself has not been improved. Instead, hype has been used to artificially inflate the price. Rather than the price of land being determined by the value of the asset erected on the property, value is determined by how well a realtor markets the asset.

It is not simply a case of the landlord negotiating with a prospective buyer. Instead, realtors act as agents, adding a cost to the final product. In the process they ensure that they make a profit. The end result of this process is that the exchange escalates the price of ownership, which in turn means that landlords demand higher rents for their investments. Meanwhile, the rental units themselves have not been improved, and the added value results from artificial means.

Rental units are being created for individuals who cannot afford a home, but are able to pay high rents. Speculators are able to profit from developing rental housing for this segment of the rental market. On the other hand, speculation for the low end of the market is usually less profitable. City governments have often supported speculation. Lorimer (1978) has observed:

> The consequence of this arrangement, however, is that the corporate city and its interlocking pieces are designed not to provide a humane and livable city, but rather to maximize the profits to be made from urban land and to capture as much control over the process of urban growth as possible for the development of industry. (p. 79)

The notion of created value is consistent with tax laws designed to further the interests of the wealthy (Feagin 1986). For example, in New York City, developers bought up older but still functional office buildings, tore them down, and constructed new ones (Meyer 1979). This obviously wasteful practice was very profitable to developers because the old office buildings were fully depreciated, whereas new construction could benefit from depreciation. This same rationale has been used by developers to convert older but still functional apartments into condominiums.

Banks and Speculation

Speculation is also used to create and maintain slums. For example, developers in Washington, D.C. bought up properties and sold them to professionals for the tax write-off (Downie 1974). The new buyers had a disincentive to upgrade these properties because they purchased them solely as a means of reducing taxes from their professional practices. After the properties are fully depreciated and the professionals realize their maximum profit, the units are gentrified for up-scale buyers. Rather than advocate against such practices, some city governments have actually supported gentrification by improving parks and streets, and by providing below-market financing (Clay 1979).

Suburban areas are also subject to speculation. Developers and speculators buy up farm land to build new homes, which in turn raises taxes on agriculture land. As a result, farmers find it unprofitable and sell their land. What was once agricultural land is quickly turned into higher-priced subdivided lots.

Banks and other financial institutions profit by loaning as much as 80 to 90 percent of the mortgages that finance speculation. This in turn drives up the price of eventual construction. Oftentimes, speculators will purchase homes at below-market prices that been foreclosed by banks. These purchases will be made with government-backed mortgage funds that are supported by tax dollars. As a result, speculators are able to increase their profits by as much as 50 percent by obtaining funds at below-market rates—a subsidy supported by the American taxpayer. These homes will then be quickly sold and the price of housing increased.

Large corporations have now entered this speculation process, and quickly drive out smaller firms. Profit margins are quickly squeezed, and new construction is further inflated.

Speculation depends, in part, on the ability of financial institutions to effectively manipulate real estate markets. If you are a renter or home owner in an area targeted by the bank for withdrawal of its financial support, this process amounts to disinvestment (Harvey 1975). Some investors choose to hold on and undermaintain their properties with the hope that they can continue to reap profits until they sell. Other investors quickly sell their properties and move on to the area selected by the banks as a potentially profitable market. Communities where disinvestment has occurred quickly fall victim to neglect, abandonment, theft, and deterioration. In effect, citizens in these communities are thrust into poverty by financial institutions. There are numerous examples of this process, including East Saint Louis, Illinois, Lawndale, Chicago, and sections of Washington, D.C.

From the bank's vantage point, the decision to manipulate the real estate market is rational; they must compete with other financial institutions for funds and profits. If their funds are invested in projects that pay low rates of return, their ability to attract deposits is jeopardized. The earnings squeeze of the mid-1960s illustrates this phenomenon. Because of rising interest rates, banks quickly moved to disinvest themselves of loans or potential loans that yielded low rates of return. Congress's response to this earnings squeeze was to deregulate thrifts and lift restrictions that had prevented thrifts and savings and loans from investing in consumer and commercial loans. In turn, banks invested in loans that yielded higher returns and were often highly speculative. As a result, by "1988, 350 of the nation's 3,024 insured thrift institutions were insolvent" (Brumbaugh and Litan 1989, p. 4). Scholars Brumbaugh and Litan (1989) argue against the notion that deregulation caused the current savings and loan crisis. They maintain that "lax supervision and weak capital standards" were to blame (p. 7).

The controversy over the thrift crisis reflects the bias in this nation toward tax laws and regulation that favor business and the affluent at the expense of the working class. Regulation is deemed bad if it impedes business in making a profit. However, as business begins to stumble and face financial crisis, Congress is then blamed for not more closely supervising business. Low-income individuals frequently bear the cost of few regulations. For example, Leven et al. (1976) found that savings institutions in New York demanded higher rates and less favorable terms for payments than came due on the city's rental housing stock. In some instances, banks actually required those owners who wanted to refinance their properties to convert the rental units to cooperative housing (co-ops). Bankers did this so the people requesting the loans would be in a better financial position to pay the higher interest charged by the banks. It is also important to note that an obvious consequence of this action was to force many low-income renters out of the housing market.

Finally, the supply of low-income housing has declined because of slum clearance to make room for urban renewal and gentrification. In 1980, the United States embarked on massive slum clearance in which over 735,000 households were displaced (Piven & Cloward 1987). The effect on the rental market was to force more people into fewer housing units and raise the prevailing cost of a rental unit. At the same time, conversion, gentrification, and abandonment resulted in the loss of a half a million low-rent housing units (Hartman et al. 1982).

The notion of a supply and demand curve for housing converging freely and establishing an equilibrium in which buyers and renters are able to compete fairly with sellers and landlords is obviously a myth. Instead, speculators, bankers, and developers, not the market, create prices. The poor are particularly ill-affected by this process because they lack the capital or access to capital necessary to compete effectively in a commodity-based housing market.

Social Spending for Housing:
Whom Does It Benefit?

Ira S. Lowry (1987), an economist associated with the Rand Corporation, asks the question, where should the poor live? Like many conservative scholars, Lowry views many of the poor as deviant, arguing that they choose to pay less for housing than the middle class. Charles Murray (1984), another conservative scholar, adds that the poor's imprudence and lack of judgment are to blame for their inability to afford housing. The notion that the poor do not value housing in the same way as do the middle class ignores the fact that the poor have much less income. With less income, a poor person is not able to make the same choices as is a middle-class person.

Many liberal scholars, while lamenting the fact that many of the poor are inadequately housed, ignore structural aspects in the economy, such as tax favoritism for the middle and upper classes. Ironically, affluent individuals and families receive the lion's share of housing subsidies. Lower-income groups, on the other hand, already squeezed by the pervasive decline in wages that has occurred over the last decade, receive little help from the government in the way of housing subsidies.

The growth of an underclass of people who are denied access to the political and economic mainstream has risen over the last decade. In 1959, 39.5 million people, or 22.4 percent of the population, were considered poor (U.S. Bureau of Census 1982, 1984). By 1978, that number had dropped to 11 percent. However, by 1983, the number of poor had risen to 35.3 million people, or 15.2 percent of the population. The rise in poverty is illustrated by the growing discrepancy between rents and incomes:

> In 1970, the number of rental units that rented for no more than 30 percent of the income of a household earning $10,000 a year (i.e., for no more than $250 a month) was approximately 2.4 million greater than number of renter households with incomes at or below this level. In 1985, some 11.6 million renter households . . . had incomes of $10,000 or less, but only 7.9 million units rented for $250 a month or less. (Center on Budget and Policy Priorities 1989, p. xiii)

This highlights the widening gap between incomes and rental prices. At first glance, social spending, and particularly welfare programs, are used to combat poverty. Liberals are bashed by conservatives such as Charles Murray

(1984), who argue that rising incidence of poverty shows the ineffectiveness of the massive social welfare spending of the 1960s. However, a closer examination of what is meant by social welfare spending shows that only a small percentage of this spending actually benefits the poor. Jencks (1985) observes:

> In 1980, only a fifth of all "social spending" was explicitly aimed at low-income families, and only a tenth was for programs for providing cash, food, or housing to such families. (p. 43)

Social spending includes education, military pensions, and Social Security. Many of these benefits go to the middle class. Therefore, as Piven and Cloward (1976) point out, the intent of welfare programs is designed for social control and appeasement, instead of a concentrated effort to raise people out of poverty.

In 1984, the Congressional Joint Committee on Taxation estimated the cost to the U.S. Treasury for housing-related tax write-offs at $43 trillion (Dolbeare 1986). This includes subsidies for historic structure preservation, tax-exempt rental housing bonds, five-year amortization of low-income housing rehabilitation, mortgage interest, property taxes, capital gain deferral, capital gain exclusion, and residential energy credits. Mortgage interest amounts to $44 billion annually, and 70 percent of this subsidy goes to people with incomes over $30,000 (Hartman 1987). Obviously, lower-income home owners are not the primary beneficiaries of these deductions.

The amount of tax monies used to subsidize the affluent at the expense of the poor is summed up by Cushing Dolbeare, president of the National Low Income Housing Coalition:

> Benefits from federal housing programs are so skewed that the total of all federal payments ever made under HUD programs, from the inception of public housing in 1937 through 1980, was less than the cost to the federal government of housing-related tax expenditures in 1980 alone. (Dolbeare 1983, p. 69)

In 1974, the Housing and Development Act, commonly known as Section 8, was passed. The first part of the program used rent assistance to subsidize low-income tenants. If the tenant moved, the rent assistance moved with the tenant. The second part of the program was used to construct new rental housing and also to rehabilitate existing rental housing. Landlords had to agree that the newly constructed or converted units remain in the program for twenty years. This agreement is in some ways like a time bomb. As Dreier (1987) observes:

> This ticking time bomb is a result of the shortsightedness of policy makers who, disillusioned with the public housing program in the 1950s and 1970s,

created programs to induce private for-profit developers to build low-income housing. . . . The 20 years are now up, and many owners want to cash in; in some hot housing markets an apartment, built at taxpayer's expense for $15,000 20 years ago, is now worth over $100,000 as a condominium. (p. 21)

Around 300,000 low-income units are expected to be lost as the result of the expiration of these twenty-year contracts.

In effect, Section 8 enabled developers to make a profit during the initial construction and at the end of the twenty-year contracts by taking a taxpayer-subsidized investment and converting it for their own profit. In addition, it "rapidly became a relief measure to rescue financially insecure projects under earlier programs" (Sternlieb & Listokin 1987). Many landlords have been eager to join the program because they can negotiate rent increases and avoid losses through abandonment (Rydell et al. 1980).

Meanwhile, under the Reagan administration, new housing starts for government-initiated subsidized housing dropped from 180,000 units in 1980–81 to 70,000 units in 1985. It is true that the federal government funded the Community Development Block Grant program, which provided a stimulus so local governments would then provide additional funding to rehabilitate low-cost housing. In 1982, this program created 225,000 low-income housing units nationwide (Listokin 1983). Nevertheless, the construction of low-income housing has not kept pace with the rapid destruction of the low-income housing stock.

Instead of constructing low-income housing, the federal government is increasingly using housing vouchers that are portable (move with the tenant). The decision to forgo federally constructed and managed low-income units is based on the notion that market competition will control costs, whereas bureaucratic oversight will not (President's Commission on Housing 1982). In the case of public housing, however, studies have shown that pressures to satisfy the demand for profit drove up the cost of the public housing projects (Freedman 1969; McConnell 1957). Another cost of public housing is the gross mismanagement within the U.S. Department of Housing and Urban Development (HUD). In fact, the corruption and mismanagement at HUD, in which over $500 million dollars may have been lost to fraud, resulted from ". . . draconian staff cuts, wholesale political appointments to top jobs and books in chronic disarray, HUD has been an open invitation to plundering" (Martz & Thomas 1989), p. 21.

The U.S. Department of Housing and Urban Development is projected to spend $9.8 billion for subsidized housing in fiscal year 1988. Since 1978, this represents a reduction of 80 percent. By 1987, the federal government was serving 1.4 million fewer households than they did in 1979.

Public housing has historically not been a national priority. The 1960s were an exception to this case. The Housing and Development Act of 1968 set a goal of 26 million substantially rehabilitated units over the following decade. However, in 1971, President Nixon halted all construction. The 1968 Act pledged a massive campaign to construct low-income housing and satisfied one goal of some government officials, which was to appease those demanding a redistribution of wealth for the poor.

When the federal government has sponsored public housing it has often done so in a manner designed to control unrest, rather than to provide aid. Public housing officials have been found to look down on the tenants. In a noted case, the Boston Housing Authority consistently ignored calls for repairs to the buildings.

The federal government's disdain for public housing appears to be reserved for the poor. As Hartman and Stone (1986) observe:

> Some 450,000 units of family housing have been constructed by the military, a public housing program about one-third the size of the far-better-known low-rent public housing program established by the 1937 Housing Act. (p. 487)

This housing is maintained well and there has not been a public outcry about government mismanagement, fraud, and waste. The public's general acceptance of public housing for the military as opposed to the poor underscores the heart of the housing crisis facing this nation. Unlike the poor, military personnel, even though they receive a combination of pay and benefits that far exceed benefits to the poor, are viewed as having a legitimate right to public housing. The poor, on the other hand, have not earned their tenure and are judged by many as undeserving of housing subsidies.

Alternative Solutions to the Housing Crisis

As we discussed in chapter 3, efforts that expect to raise people out of poverty or a life of persistently low wages must concentrate on incomes. At the same time, practices such as speculation and tax favoritism that make housing inaccessible to individuals and families must be eliminated.

There is little doubt that current housing policy favors the affluent and discriminates against the poor. Can a capitalist view of housing continue and homelessness be dramatically reduced, or is it necessary to shift to a socialist form of housing? Given the fact that capitalistic values are deeply entrenched in the American experience, an approach that does not uproot capitalism, but adjusts it, stands a better chance of eventually being adopted by elected officials.

It seems obvious that as long as housing is viewed as a commodity and not regulated, there will be individuals who cannot afford to purchase or even rent a home. Businesses, such as real estate firms, mortgage bankers, and developers, will continue to drive up housing costs in order to maximize their own gains. Because the consumer is not able to substitute another commodity, such as they would when the price of oranges is too high, they must either pay increased costs or become homeless.

We base our following suggestions on the premise that homelessness is unacceptable and housing is a right as opposed to a privilege. Therefore, policies and practices, such as speculation, that favor the affluent at the expense of the poor must be eliminated. Models of rational housing policy are few; however, Sweden has some of the most progressive housing policies of any developed nation. Some of Sweden's ideas are useful to review. In 1968, Swedish lawmakers enacted the Rent Act of 1968, which established a set of "key safeguards" for tenants (Appelbaum 1986, p. 543). Included in this Act was a direct bargaining arrangement between landlords' organizations and the National Tenant's Union. In addition, it was made almost impossible for landlords to convert their property into condominiums. Those landlords who decide not to maintain their properties are punished.

Other aspects of Sweden's housing policy include a system of housing allowances that reach far into the middle class (Nesslein 1982). As opposed to relying on a mortgage interest deduction, housing allowances reach a greater portion of the populace and do not stigmatize one group, such as the poor, in favor of another.

Municipalities in Sweden bank land for future development and form a king of public utility in which future rental units must be constructed on this land. The municipalities provides financing for the construction and set standards. Speculation is deterred through a capital gains tax of 75 percent on short-term gains (Headey 1978). Private housing is allowed under this system, but the loan rate on these units is higher than on publicly owned housing. This process encourages public as opposed to private rentals.

Housing policy molded after Sweden's is possible in the United States, but it is highly unlikely. A far more modest proposal to address the unequitable U.S. housing policy was made by members of Congress during the tax reform legislation debate in 1985. A $5,000 limit on interest payment deductions for a second home was proposed. The chief executive officer for the National Association of Realtors labeled it "a $300 billion destruction of value" (Hinds 1984). Attempts to redistribute wealth will undoubtedly come under attack by those whose self-interest would be threatened. Do the American people have both the inclination and will to change current housing policies that favor the affluent over the poor?

While we cannot answer this question, it is important to outline some means of achieving a rational housing policy that begins to recognize housing as a right. We offer a few modest proposals that are feasible in the American political system: first, limit the amount of interest a homeowner can deduct for a principal residence; second, redefine rent subsidies, such as under Section 8, as ownership subsidies; third, tax all exchanges of property including similar exchanges, and raise the short-term capital gains tax rate; fourth, create a commission composed of tenants, landlords, and residents in the community to set rents; fifth, require realtors to advertise their rates and begin antitrust action for price fixing against associations of realtors; sixth, eliminate points charged by banks to consumers to secure loans; seventh, charge landlords strict fines for not maintaining their property; eighth supplement the national housing stock annually with government constructed and owned housing; and finally, ninth, offer mortgages from the government that are two points below the prevailing market rate of interest.

Limits on Home Owner Deductions

The limit on the amount of interest home owners could deduct for their principal residence could fund the ownership subsidies. Currently, there is a limit on home mortgage interest; however, that limit applies only to a *$1 million residence.* While it is promising that legislators have finally set a limit on home mortgage interest, the cap continues to discriminate in favor of the affluent at the expense of the poor. Studies have shown that a reduction in the home mortgage interest deduction could easily fund a housing entitlement program (Downs 1973). In 1987, about 75 percent of the housing-related tax expenditures went to people whose incomes were in the top 15 percent nationally (Center on Budget and Policy Priorities 1989). In effect, the federal government is aiding the affluent in their efforts to develop and maintain assets. As noted by some scholars, such as Sheradeen (1988), one of the best means to help the poor escape poverty is to enable them to also develop and maintain assets.

A potential criticism of this approach is that a cap on the home mortgage interest deduction would unnecessarily damage the housing industry and reduce the assets of those who own more expensive homes. Certainly, the housing industry, particularly those builders who constructed homes for more affluent buyers, would go through a period of adjustment in which some firms would suffer financial collapse.

Should the government bail out these firms and, if so, how should the compensation be determined? Obviously, it would be unfair to punish developers for being successful at building a product—up-scale housing—that the economy had in the past favored. However, compensation should be determined by examining the developer's initial investment and the current resale value of that investment. The United States should not make the same mistake as France, which bailed out firms at their fair-market value and then realized that the assets purchased were often in need of significant repairs.

While on one hand it is reasonable to compensate developers for actual invest-ment that is lost, it would be both expensive and wasteful to compensate developers for more than an asset is actually worth.

The charge that affluent home owners would lose a portion of their investment also is reasonable. They too should be compensated. Once again, it is important to do so in a way that compensates for actual investment and not for expected appreciation. One way to accomplish this goal is to phase-in over five years the cap on home mortgage interest. At the end of the five years, home owners would be able to deduct a one-time charge, determined by calculating the purchase price of the home, the rate of inflation over the period of ownership, and the amount lost as a result of not being able to deduct the interest on the home above the cap, against current earned income.

Ownership Issues

The conversion of Section 8 vouchers from rent subsidies to purchase cer-tificates redistributes wealth from the more affluent to the poor. The notion of purchase certificates enables the poor to participate in the housing market. They are able to use these funds to make a down-payment and subsidize a portion of their monthly mortgage payment.

Much of the revenue needed to fund this program can be obtained from placing a cap on the home mortgage interest deduction. Another way to ob-tain revenues would be to reduce the depreciation for rental housing. Since housing, in general, actually appreciates, reducing the amount of the depreciation allowance should not hurt investment.

One of the obvious effects of using purchase certificates instead of rent vouchers is that demand for low-income homes will increase. At the same time, some rental units will become unprofitable. Once again, this program should be phased-in over five years to enable landlords to adjust and to enable developers to shift from constructing more affluent to more modest homes.

An interesting approach that we have not addressed is one favored by the Institute for Policy Studies Working Group on Housing (1989). This group favors conversion to social ownership, in which homeowners could sell their properties to the government and then receive a stipend for the value of the property and live in the property. This approach has many strengths, such as enabling many households to avoid displacement; however, over time more housing would be removed from the private sector and placed in the hands of the government. One negative effect of this approach is that since the homes are not owned and we live in a market-driven economy, occupant motivation to maintain them might decrease. Given the fact that we operate in a market-oriented society, any approach toward reforming housing must work within these parameters.

Limitations on Short-Term Capital Gains

Currently, real estate exchanges are such that someone exchanges one piece of property for another and pays tax on any amount that is greater than the price of the property being exchanged. Under the current tax laws, all short-term gains are taxed at the normal rate an individual would pay, which is a maximum of 33 percent. We propose reinstating a short-term capital gains tax rate of 75 percent on all exchanges of property or assets. Critics would be quick to charge that such a high short-term rate would discourage investment and slow down the economy. On the contrary; our approach would simply discourage short-term investments in favor of long-term investments.

Commission to Control Rents

Better control of the rental market is desperately needed to reduce displacement. There is a myth that rents are set by invisible market forces that seek an equilibrium. However, we have already shown that rents are more often determined by factors such as the prevailing interest rate for mortgages and other investment opportunities like stocks and bonds. A process whereby commissions composed of landlords and tenants bargain over rent increases provides less chance for landlords to charge whatever they wish. The commission would have the force of law to mandate rent increases and penalize landlords who charged more than the mandated increase.

Critics of this approach charge that if a landlord could receive a higher rate of return in the stock market, a commission-determined as opposed to a market-determined rent could unfairly penalize the landlord. This criticism is reasonable; therefore, landlords could choose to sell their properties to the government. Fair compensation would be determined by a formula similar to that proposed for developers. It would not, however, be "fair market value." The landlords, instead of basing their decisions on short-term considerations, will be more likely to consider the long-term potentials of their investments.

Antitrust Action Against Realty Associations

We next need to consider ways of reducing the cost of purchasing a home. One of the costs seldom mentioned when purchasing a house is the cost the realtors charge the sellers for their services. As a result, the price of a home can rise as much as 10 percent. This is not to suggest that realtors do not provide actual and meaningful services. The market does not determine the value of these services, but instead, realtors' fees are determined and maintained by associations of realtors. Therefore, antitrust action against the real estate industry seems not only just, but necessary to effect broader access to consumers.

Reducing the Cost of Borrowing

Also important is to eliminate points charged by banks for loans. Banks maintain that it is expensive for them to lend money, and the points are a justifiable cost of the time needed to process the loan. In actuality, points are a way for the bank to charge a higher interest rate and avoid criticism that their interest rates are excessive. One of the best ways to resolve this controversy is to establish a commission to examine how much it actually costs a bank to process a loan application, and allow banks to charge for those costs. Since the bank makes money on the loan, a reasonable cost to process the loan would be not over $250.

Requiring Maintenance from Landlords

The notion that landlords should be able to maintain their properties in any way they deem appropriate is simply unacceptable. One of the criticisms of efforts to mandate that landlords maintain their properties is that they would be unduly burdened by excessive and unnecessary governmental meddling. As has already been noted, landlords in general are interested in extracting as much profit as possible from their holdings. This creates an added incentive for landlords to do as little as possible in the way of maintenance. Otherwise, their potential cash flow would be diminished. Laws that attach a significant financial penalty and vigorously enforce compliance would add a disincentive to landlords who do not maintain their properties. In fact, those who do not maintain their properties would face diminished cash flows as a result of the *high* financial penalties.

Increasing National Housing Stock

As long as housing is viewed as a commodity, there will be a need for the government to increase the national housing stock through the creation of public housing. However, unlike current efforts, the creation of government subsidized housing need not be done in a shoddy manner so the costs are high and the resulting management is wasteful and mean-spirited. First, government housing for the poor should be constructed along the same lines as housing for the military. The current system by which HUD subsidizes private construction of low-income housing is a give-away program for the affluent because, rather than becoming part of the housing infrastructure, subsidized housing eventually reverts to the private sector. Housing vouchers, in which low-income individuals rent units in the private sector, are expensive and only add temporarily to the low-income housing stock.

The second issue in the construction and management of low-income housing is to insist that management personnel hold degrees in urban studies, social work, or community planning. In addition, personnel should reflect the composition of residents who live in the housing. The current practice of hiring individuals from the business sector is somewhat paradoxical in that these individuals are generally not sympathetic to the plight of public housing tenants.

The federal government should also develop land banks in which abandoned and condemned properties are placed into the public trust for the construction of public housing. Currently, local communities sell these properties to the highest bidder, and they remain in the market sector. Our approach would withdraw these properties from the private sector.

A commitment to the construction and maintenance of public housing has *never* been tried in this country. Therefore, criticisms of this approach that point to the current state of affairs in public housing are irrelevant.

Provision of Government Mortgages

Currently, the government guarantees loans made by private banks through the Federal Housing Administration (FHA). These loans have been helpful in enabling many buyers to afford housing. Unfortunately, the program does not go far enough in creating mortgages that are affordable. We suggest that tax monies be set aside and placed in a trust that could then be loaned to qualified buyers. Unlike with the current FHA program, the funds would be generated by tax revenues and would not depend on the private market. Banks could sell these mortgages, yet the government would charge banks for this privilege.

The provision of mortgage money by the government does compete with private banking interests. However, this competition will lower the prevailing mortgage interest rate. Instead of competing in the open money market for funds to finance these mortgages, the government would use a percentage of tax revenues that will be generated by a higher marginal tax rate. This process redistributes assets from the affluent to the poor and enables more individuals to participate in the mainstream economy. It also prevents mortgage rates from rising.

In Summary

Our suggestions offer the elements of a housing policy designed to move the country toward recognizing housing as a right. These alternatives are not as far-reaching or as broad-based as those found in Sweden. Nevertheless, they do challenge entrenched values, such as an individual's supreme right to use an asset however he or she wishes. Do our proposals go far enough? To many, such as the National Association of Realtors, our proposals smack of unbridled socialism. On the other hand, to some homeless advocates, our proposals do not go far enough in improving the ability of the poor to afford adequate housing.

Obviously, efforts to resolve the housing crisis require hard choices that challenge entrenched values. Home ownership is one such value. On one hand, our efforts to increase wages are designed to enable more Americans to participate in the economic mainstream. On the other hand, this process will not result in all Americans being able to afford housing. Two questions must be resolved to address this inequity: first, what is our responsibility, as a society, for the housing needs of these individuals?; and second, do we, as society, want to abandon the goal of home ownership? These unsettling questions are not easily resolved.

It is interesting how liberals in particular lament the housing crisis but shy away from approaches that both redistribute wealth and end middle to upper income tax favoritism, such as the mortgage interest deduction. Basically, we are arguing that the poor have a right to participate in the mainstream economy. This approach is, however, threatening to those who alredy consider themselves part of the privileged class and to those who believe they can make it into the privileged class. Many of the poor are under no such illusion, for they are homeless.

We suggest the most equitable solution to this dilemma is to lower the cost of home ownership, increase home ownership assistance to more Americans through the use of credits and not deductions, and create government-subsidized, low-income housing for those who are unable to purchase a home. In order to guarantee the success of this approach, the federal government will have to ensure that enough housing is developed in both the private and public sectors to prevent shortages in either.

Future efforts to address the shortage of housing in this country for low-income Americans must wrestle with the issue of the ability of the economy to produce enough good jobs so that more Americans can afford housing. However, the present imbalance in favor of those with higher incomes means that significant income redistribution will have to accompany approaches that favor an increase in the types of employment that provide higher incomes. It is the continuing resistance to the redistribution of income, however, that makes any meaningful attempt to address the housing crisis doubtful.

Thus far we have addressed the needs of individuals who are not handicapped by a mental disability. There are many homeless individuals who suffer from chronic mental illness. Addressing their needs is the subject of the next chapter.

References

Appelbaum, R.P. (1986). Swedish housing in the postwar period: Some lessons for American housing policy. In Bratt, R.G., Hartman, C. & Meyerson, A. (eds),

Critical Perspectives on Housing. Philadelphia: Temple University Press, 535–58.

Appelbaum, R.P. & Glasser, T. (1982). *Concentration of Ownership in Isla Vista, California*. Santa Barbara, CA: UCSB Housing Office.

Appelbaum, R.P. & Gilderbloom, J.I. (1986). Supply-side economics and rents: Are rental housing markets truly competitive? In Bratt, R.G., Hartman, C. & Meyerson, A. (eds), *Critical Perspectives on Housing*. Philadelphia: Temple University Press, 165–79.

Belcher, J.R. & Singer, J. (1988). Homelessness: A cost of capitalism. *Social Policy, 18,* (4): 44–48.

Brumbaugh, R.D. & Litan, R.E. (1989). The S & L crisis: How to get out and stay out. *The Brookings Review, 7,* (2): 3–13.

Center on Budget and Policy Priorities (1989). *A Place to Call Home: The Crisis in Housing for the Poor*. Washington, D.C.: Low Income Housing Information Service.

Clay, P. (1979). *Neighborhood Renewal*. Lexington, MA: D.C. Heath.

Dolbeare, C. (1983). The low income housing crisis. In Hartman, C. (ed.), *America's Housing Crisis: What Is to Be Done?* Boston: Routledge & Kegan Paul.

———. (1986). How the income tax subsidizes housing for the affluent. In Bratt, R.G., Hartman, C. & Meyerson, A. (eds), *Critical Perspectives on Housing*. Philadelphia: Temple University Press, 264–71.

Downie, L. (1974). *Mortgage on America*. New York: Praeger.

Downs, A. (1973). *Federal Housing Subsidies: How Are They Working?* Lexington, MA: D.C. Heath.

Dreier, P. (1987). Community-based housing: A progressive approach to a new federal policy. *Social Policy, 17,* 18–22.

Feagin, J.R. (1986). Urban real estate speculation in the United States: Implications for social science and urban planning. In Bratt, R.G., Hartman, C. & Meyerson, A. (eds), *Critical Perspectives on Housing*. Philadelphia: Temple University Press., 99–118.

Freedman, L. (1969). *Public Housing: The Politics of Poverty*. New York: Holt, Rinehart & Winston.

Gelfand, M. (1975). *A Nation of Cities: The Federal Government and Urban America 1933–1965*. New York: Oxford University Press.

Gilderbloom, J.I. & Keating, D. (1982). *An Evaluation of Rent Control in Orange, New Jersey*. Santa Barbara, CA: Foundation for National Progress, Housing Information Center.

Gray, T. (1979). *Student Housing and Discrimination*. Santa Barbara, CA: University of California Press.

Hartman, C. (1987). The housing part of the homelessness problem. In *Homelessness: Critical Issues for Policy and Practice*. Boston: The Boston Foundation.

Hartman, C., Keating, D. & LeGates, R. (1982). *Displacement: How to Fight It*. Berkeley, CA: National Housing Law Project.

Hartman, C. & Stone, M.E. (1986). A socialist housing alternative for the United States. In Bratt, R.G., Hartman, C. & Meyerson, A. (eds.). *Critical Perspectives on Housing*. Philadelphia: Temple University Press.

Harvey, D. (1975). The political economy of urbanization in advanced capitalist societies: The case of the United States. In Gappert, G. (ed), *The Social Economy of Cities: Urban Affairs Annual Review*. Beverly Hills: Sage.

Headey, B. (1978). *Housing Policy in the Developed Economy*. London: Croom Helm.

Hinds, M.D. (1984). Tax plan clouds future for homeowners and investors. *New York Times,* December 30.

Hopper, K. & Hamberg, J. (1986). The making of America's homeless: From skid row to new poor, 1945–1984. In Bratt, R.G., Hartman, C. & Meyerson, A. (eds.), *Critical Perspectives on Housing*. Philadelphia: Temple University Press, 12–40.

H.R. 286, 101th Congress (1987). January 6.

Institute for Policy Studies Working Group on Housing (1989). *The Right to Housing: A Blueprint for Housing the Nation*. Washington, D.C.: Institute for Policy Studies.

Jencks, C. (1985). How poor are the poor? *The New York Review of Books,* May 9, 41–9.

Kuttner, R. (1984). *The Economic Illusion*. Boston: Houghton Mifflin.

Leven, C., Little, J., Nourse, H., & Read, R. (1976). Neighborhood change: Lessons in the dynamics of urban decay. In *Housing in America: Problems and Perspectives*. Montgomery, R. & Mandelker, D.R. (eds.), 2d ed. New York: Bobbs-Merrill.

Linson, N. (1978). *Concentration of Ownership in Santa Barbara*. Santa Barbara, CA: Foundation for National Progress, Housing Information Center.

Listokin, D. (1983). *Housing Rehabilitation: Economic, Social and Policy Perspectives*. New Brunswick, NJ: Rutgers University, Center for Urban Policy Research.

Lorimer, J. (1978). *The Developers*. Toronto: James Lorimer.

Lowry, I.S. (1987). Where should the poor live? In Salins, P.D. (Ed.), *Housing America's Poor*. Chapel Hill, NC: The University of North Carolina Press.

Martz, L. & Thomas, R. (1989). Still more scandals at HUD. *Newsweek,* July 21, 3.

McDonnell, T. (1957). *The Wagner Housing Act: A Case Study of the Legislative Process*. Chicago: Layola University Press.

Meyer, P. (1979). Land Rush. *Harper's 258* (January): 45–60.

Murray, C. (1984). *Losing Ground: American Social Policy, 1950–1980*. New York: Basic Books, Inc.

Nesslein, T.S. (1982). The Swedish housing model: An assessment. *Urban Studies,* 19, 235–46.

Piven, F.F. & Cloward, R.A. (1987). The contemporary relief debate. In Block, F., Cloward, R.A., Ehrenreich, B. & Piven, F.F., *The Mean Season*. New York: Pantheon Books, 45–108.

Piven, F.F. & Cloward, R.A. (1976). *Regulating the Poor: The Functions of Public Welfare*. New York: Vintage Books.

President's Commission on Housing (1982). *The Report of the President's Commission on Housing*. Washington, D.C.: Government Printing Office.

Quigley, J.M. (1979). What have we learned about urban housing markets? In Mieszkowski, P. & Straszheim, M. (eds.), *Current Issues in Urban Economics*. Baltimore: Johns Hopkins University Press.

Rydell, C., Mulford, J.E. & Helbers, L. (1980). *Price Increases Caused by Housing Assistance Programs*. Santa Monica, CA: Rand Corporation, R–2677–HUD.

Schmid, R.E. (1989). Housing gap widens for young. *The Baltimore Sun,* J1.

Scott, M. (1971). *American City Planning Since 1890.* Berkeley and Los Angeles: University of California Press.

Sheradeen, M.W. (1988). Rethinking social welfare: Toward Assets. *Social Policy, 34,* 5–9.

Sternlieb, G. & Listokin, D. (1987). A review of national housing policy. In Salins, D. (ed.), *Housing America's Poor.* Chapel Hill, NC: The University of North Carolina Press, 14–44.

Stone, M.E. (1980–81). The housing problem in the United States: Origins and prospects. *Socialist Review, 52,* (July–August): 65–119.

Stone, M.E. (1986). Housing and the dynamics of U.S. capitalism. In Bratt, R.G., Hartman, C. & Meyerson, A. (eds), *Critical Perspectives on Housing.* Philadelphia: Temple University Press, 41–67.

Stone, M.E. (1973). Federal housing policy: A political-economic analysis. In Pynoos, J., Schafer, R. & Hartman, C. (eds.), *Housing Urban America.* Chicago: Aldine.

U.S. Bureau of Census (1982). Statistical Abstract of the United States: 1982–83. Washington, D.C.: Government Printing Office.

U.S. Bureau of Census (1984). Money income and poverty status of families and persons in the United States: 1983. Washington, D.C.: Government Printing Office, Ser. P–60, No. 145.

U.S. Congress, Congressional Budget Office (1981). *The Tax Treatment of Home Ownership: Issues and Options.* Washington, D.C.: Government Printing Office.

Weicher, J.C. (1987). Private production: Has the rising tide lifted all boats? In Salins, P.D. (ed.), *Housing America's Poor.* Chapel Hill, NC: The University of North Carolina Press, 45–66.

6
Homeless and Mentally Ill: Abandoned in the Streets

E stimates of the percentage of homeless people who are mentally ill vary, yet scholars do agree that the number is growing. Is homelessness primarily a mental health problem? Some scholars have argued that increased mental health services are a major way of addressing the homeless crisis (Bassuk et al. 1984). We argue, however, that economic dislocation is the major cause of homelessness. Nevertheless, in the final analysis, preventing homelessness requires both increased mental health services and efforts to prevent economic dislocation.

Estimates suggest that approximately 30 to 40 percent of the homeless population is mentally ill (Arce & Vergare 1984; Belcher & Toomey 1987). Of these individuals, the majority suffer from chronic mental illness. The *chronically mentally ill* (CMI) are generally defined as individuals diagnosed with organic disorders, schizophrenic disorders, major affective disorders, paranoid disorders, and other psychotic disorders (Goldman 1984). Many individuals afflicted with these mental disorders are so disabled that they are unable to productively participate in society. In addition, the disability is generally prolonged and functional.

The CMI were once primarily treated in the nation's state hospitals. Today the majority reside in the community. Many, because of an exacerbation of their symptoms, will need hospitalization from time to time. Despite this fact, society has chosen to restrict their ability to receive needed hospitalization. As a result, many CMI receive no hospital care or inadequate care because they are dependent on Medicaid or an overcrowded state hospital system (Belcher 1988a). What set of circumstances has contributed to this nation turning its back on the needs of the CMI? In this chapter we examine this question and offer alternatives to the present policy of denying CMI access to hospitals.

Troubled and on the Streets

It is no mystery why so many of the CMI are homeless. Mental health policy makers have historically failed to appreciate that the severity of chronic mental illnesses, such as schizophrenia, can change rapidly over time and leave patients unable to care for themselves (Ciompi 1980). Instead of recognizing the potential for lifelong and debilitating problems resulting from chronic mental illnesses, mental health policy makers have preferred to conceptualize the chronically mentally ill as suffering from transitory problems of an acute nature. As a result, policies and theories of practice, such as deinstitutionalization, have been poorly designed and implemented. In the final analysis, mental health policy has been guided by principles of cost containment (Bevilacqua & Noble 1987), and clinical reality has seldom been considered relevant.

This is illustrated by the continuing bias in favor of community services at the expense of hospital-based services. Whereas numerous studies have noted the importance of high-quality community services for the CMI (Anthony et al. 1988), few studies highlight the need for well-staffed and clinically sound public inpatient services. Instead, the state hospital continues to be blamed for underfunded community facilities and for the large numbers of CMI among the homeless (Okin 1984). In fact, the state hospital has been compared to a prison or worse (Steffan 1985; Uhler 1986).

It is both naive and cruel to deny hospitalization to individuals who are, from time to time, in need of sanctuary and inpatient care. Our failure, as a society, to adequately provide this care has resulted in urban nomads who wander about the streets with their rights intact, but unable to exercise these rights (Belcher 1988b). Commitment laws are so narrowly interpreted that many of the CMI enjoy their legal right to remain free but are denied any right to treatment.

The model of economic dislocation discussed in this book is also applicable to the chronically mentally ill. However, their dislocation has resulted from their inability to be self-sufficient because of the severity of their illness and the unwillingness of legislators, both state and federal, to adequately fund programs. Underfunded programs are a fact of life for the CMI in both the community and in the hospital. We argue that raiding one source (the hospital) to fund the other (the community) has created a system of care in which many patients are prematurely discharged from the hospital. Once in the community, the fact that many are better, but often still unable to function, means that community treatment is difficult to successfully implement. The roots of this problem can be found in the 1960s.

The 1963 Community Mental Health Center (CMHC) Act

During the 1960s, reformers, including civil rights attorneys, mental health professionals, concerned citizens, and fiscal conservatives such as state legislators, became convinced that the nation's state mental hospitals were in desperate need of change. However, each group had a different agenda on what changes were necessary. Many supporters, such as mental health professionals, saw the need for more community support. Others, such as state legislators, were more interested in depopulating their overcrowded and underfunded state hospitals. Thus, while there was consensus that state hospital populations should be reduced, responsibility for patients when they left the hospital was not determined.

State hospitals, despite their shortcomings, had traditionally served the unwanted patient. Morrissey and Goldman (1984) observe:

> [I]n the absence of specific treatments, mental illnesses remained chronic illnesses and state hospitals remained predominantly chronic care facilities providing long-term care for poor and disabled persons. (p. 788)

Many reformers simply overlooked the fact that patients in state hospitals were often unable to work because of their illness and had no financial resources to provide for their own care. Instead, many supporters of the 1963 initiative operated under a naive belief that the private market would provide care for the chronically mentally ill.

President Kennedy established an Interagency Committee on Mental Health and unofficially appointed Boisfeuillet ("Bo") Jones to be its chairman. An issue that was never sufficiently resolved was the funding of the 500 community mental health centers proposed by the Committee on Mental Health. Secretary of Health, Education and Welfare, Anthony J. Celebrezze, argued that a "diversity of state, local, and private sources" would rapidly take the place of "temporary federal subsidies" (Foley & Sharfstein 1983, p. 51).

President Kennedy disagreed and opted to have the states support their own Community Mental Health Centers (CMHCs). However, the CMHCs were not a state initiative. Therefore, Kennedy wanted the states to pay for a system that was designed and implemented by the federal government. At the same time, Kennedy was confronted with the fact that southern state legislatures were not in agreement with civil rights and mental health initiatives. Rather than run the risk of resistance from southern states, Kennedy made the fateful decision to bypass the states and place operational control of the CMHCs in the hands of local citizen boards. Meanwhile, the Kennedy administration was telling states that they were closely considering the recommendation by the Joint Commission that a united effort take place between all levels of government (Foley & Sharfstein 1983).

One of Kennedy's major agendas was to enlist the support of various key actors, such as the American Medical Association (AMA). The AMA stressed that a fee-for-service system paid for by third-party payers, among others, should support the CMHCs. This placed pressure on the administration to make sure that the CMHCs were not directly funded by the federal government because to the AMA such a funding scheme undercut the notion of free enterprise and the traditional market system.

Jones summed up the administration's proposal:

> So what we are really advocating, Mr. Chairman, is, in a sense, removing the care of the mentally ill from a complete, almost complete, responsibility of the state through tax funds and direct operations in these isolated large state mental institutions, and putting this care back in the community to be financed and supported through the *traditional* patterns of medical care to which we have become accustomed in this country. (Hearings 1963, p. 97)

The "bold new approach" proposed by President Kennedy in many ways disenfranchised the CMI. Kennedy and his policy makers were determined to distance themselves from the overburdened and apparently inefficient state hospital system. However, factors that contributed to the state hospitals between 1903 and 1950 becoming vast warehouses were overlooked. The failure of the state hospital system can be traced, in part, to the market system of traditional medical care that refused to serve the vast majority of indigent cases. Instead, these individuals were often shifted to state hospitals. Grob (1983) points out that despite their very real shortcomings and failures, "state hospitals did provide minimum levels of care not otherwise available for individuals unable to survive for themselves" (p. 788). The fact that survival in a capitalistic nation is dependent on the ability to work was largely ignored by many who supported the final CMHC compromise.

Around this same time, chloraprimizine was introduced as a miracle drug that could cure schizophrenia. Many mental health professionals oversold the benefits of this drug to President Kennedy and led him to believe that patients on this drug would no longer need intensive services, such as commitment to a state hospital (Gronfein 1985). A troublesome issue that has never been resolved is the extent to which mental health professionals believed that drugs, such as chloraprimizine, would cure patients with schizophrenia and allow them to work. Also unresolved is what these professionals meant by "cure." Dr. Overholser of St. Elizabeth's Hospital appears to have expressed the prevailing view:

> It is not only a question of emptying the hospital or reducing the load, not only restoring the patient to his family, but making him a *productive* unit in society. (Hearings 1955, p. 12)

Was there evidence to the contrary? Researchers found that some CMI individuals could develop significant problems; however, these findings were largely ignored by many in the mental health establishment (Passamanick et al. 1967).

The Joint Commission on Health and Mental Illness recognized the vulnerability of the CMI and recommended federal aid to reform the state hospital system. The National Institute of Mental Health under the direction of Robert Felix chose to ignore the Commission's recommendations for reform of the state hospital system. In particular, the National Institute of Health and the National Advisory Mental Health Council did not favor a federal role in direct-care patient costs (Foley & Sharfstein 1983). This fateful decision set the stage for the dumping of thousands of CMI into the streets with little or no community support. As noted later in this chapter, CMHCs were unprepared to handle the problems of former hospitalized patients.

On October 31, 1963, President Kennedy signed into law the CMHC Act. The final compromise legislation provided money only for the construction of community facilities. Money was not appropriated to reform state hospitals or for direct patient care costs in CMHCs. Later legislation provided money for initial staffing in CMHCs. Many of the CMI, however, did not fair well from either of these pieces of legislation. State hospitals were encouraged to discharge their patients, but community care was woefully underfunded. The abandonment of the CMI seemed to be based on the naive assumption that states would provide adequate funding necessary to operate both the CMHC system and the state hospital system. This logic, however, contradicted the fact that state legislatures across the country had historically grossly underfunded programs for the CMI. As should have been predicted, reform in state hospitals did not take place, and state governments, through their state hospital systems, continued to receive and house society's unwanted.

Civil rights advocates, particularly some within the legal establishment, played an active role in the depopulation of state hospitals by viewing the chronically mentally ill as not being ill (Bostick et al. 1983; Scheff 1984). Instead, they appeared to assume that once the CMI were released from state hospitals, former patients could resume lives in which they would not be in danger of future decompensation. Therefore, voluntary admission was made almost impossible at state institutions, and involuntary commitment was narrowed to the point that patients had to be *overtly* suicidal or homicidal (Wanck 1984).

Rather than question the priorities of individual groups to determine if potential conflicts would arise, mental health professionals, lawyers, state legislators, and advocates for the mentally ill endorsed the CMHC legislation of 1963. As a result, the back door to state hospitals was thrown open as patients were quickly discharged into ill-prepared CMHCs and nonexistent community facilities, and the front door was shut, with only a toehold left open, as the succeeding years were used to further narrow admission criteria and civil commitment statutes (Durham 1985).

The notion that the CMI were not in fact suffering from chronic mental illness was operationalized in the 1963 CMHC legislation by focusing on patients in the community who had never been hospitalized. These new patients were not considered chronic, and it was believed that they would rapidly recover from their mental health problems. The fact that chronic mental illness was present in both the community and in the state hospital was overlooked. More important, many appeared to believe that state institutions were the cause of much chronic mental illness. In fact, Foley and Sharfstein (1983) observe:

> CMHCs were originally intended to serve new constituencies in their own communities [rather] than large numbers of a great under-constituency of patients discharged "better but not well" from mental institutions to communities. (p. 101)

In 1972, Supplemental Social Security Income (SSI) was passed, and state legislators, historically noted for their fiscal conservativeness, realized an opportunity to discharge more patients into the community. Medicaid and Title XX funds did pay for the cost of some community care; however, because Medicaid reimbursed hospitals at lower rates than other insurance providers, such as Blue Cross, many of the CMI remained dependent on the state hospital for their inpatient care.

Where did the former patients of state hospitals go when they were discharged? By the late 1970s, it was apparent that many CMHCs were not prepared to handle the problems of CMIs who had never been institutionalized. A writer in 1978 observed:

> Once discharged from the total institution, the asylum, they often arrive in hostile communities with a nonsystem of care supported by a bewildering array of federal, state, and local programs making up a confusing patchwork of services and financing. (Sharfstein & Clark 1978, p. 413)

Similar reports prompted the General Accounting Office to observe in 1978: "deinstitutionalization of the mentally ill has been plagued by the lack of a planned, well managed, coordinated and systematic approach" (General Accounting Office 1978, p. 13). Scholars noted that the depopulation of state hospitals simply occurred with little coordination between the states and new CMHCs (Bassuk & Gerson 1978; Chu & Trotter 1974).

Homelessness and the Chronically Mentally Ill

By the late 1970s and early 1980s, the CMI began to appear among the homeless in increasing numbers. Many ended up in jail (Lamb & Grant 1982; Teplin 1983), others ended up on the streets. Debates ensued over how the CMI became homeless. Some scholars noted the continued funding of the state hospital and pointed out that dollars were not following patients (Brown 1983; Okin 1985). If the state hospital was destroyed, it was argued, then the community could receive adequate funding.

This view, however, failed to grasp the fact that many, if not the majority, of the CMI are not fully capable of community living and will experience from time to time a significant exacerbation of their symptoms (Harrow et al. 1983). Despite the best efforts of the community, these periods of decompensation will require a respite of some type in which the patients can remove themselves from the stresses of the community.

Despite studies that have concluded that hospitals are necessary in the continuum of care for the CMI (Lamb 1984; Appleby & Desai 1985), calls for the destruction of the state hospital continue. Much like the reforms of 1963, current efforts focus on mainstreaming the CMI into the traditional medical care system.

Privatization and Mental Health Care

Privatization is described by its supporters as providing quality, but cost-effective, interventions (Harbin & Anderson 1988). Also important to note is that much like past mental health initiatives, including deinstitutionalization, it promises that a revolutionary treatment in the community will improve the lives of the CMI. The thrust of the plan is to divert hospital admissions from state facilities to private hospital beds in the community. Therefore, on one hand it does recognize the need for hospitalization in the continuum of care for the CMI, but on the other hand, hospital beds are of little use if access is restricted to the least sick, best behaved, best insured, and least costly to serve.

The fact that the CMI have traditionally been unable to compete in a market system dominated by healthier and better-paying patients highlights the fallacy of using the private sector to care for the CMI. Supporters of privatization, much like mental health planners in the 1960s, have apparently overlooked the debilitating nature of chronic mental illness. As a result, the CMI are undergoing a further disenfranchisement.

Inherent in efforts to privatize is the urge to shift fiscal responsibility to another funding source (Belcher, in press). The 1963 CMHC act, even though it bypassed the state political process, temporarily satisfied the needs of fiscal conservatives to curtail patient care liabilities. However, state mental health expenditures have doubled, from $2.67 billion to $5.57 billion, over the last decade, with the largest percentage of this increase occurring in state institutions (Andrulis & Mazade 1983). Already experiencing fiscal pressure as the result of Reagan era budget cuts, state legislatures once again have turned to state hospitals in search of ways to reduce their cost.

Interestingly, efforts to privatize are merely renewing the historic tug-of-war between the states and the federal government over who should pay for the care of the CMI. This is not surprising given the fact that "the chronically mentally ill patient has always been an economic liability to some (level of) government" (Belcher 1988c, p. 79) because, in the end, the CMI are generally unable to support themselves. States, such as Maryland, in their haste to switch the CMI to another funding source, in this case federally supported Medicaid, run the risk of exposing the CMI who need hospitalization to the indignity of receiving no hospitalization and becoming homeless.

The decision to shift responsibility to the private sector is consistent with the philosophy of the Reagan era in which the state or federal government is viewed, by many, as not being capable of providing *cost-efficient* services. Instead, many argue that market forces are the best way to deliver services. As already noted, however, the CMI are generally unable to compete within a market-driven system because of inadequate funding, severity of illness, and odd behaviors. Can the market provide more cost-efficient services, or is this simply a value that is deeply entrenched in the American experience? An even more important question—is the market willing to accommodate and adapt to the needs of the CMI?

Despite the fact that the federal government through Medicaid will pay for much of the care, the private hospital has to manage the program so it does not incur bad debt. In the case of the CMI, however, given the long-term nature of their illness and their tendency to lack sufficient community resources, the cost of care is generally higher than with patients who are less ill, employed, and able to care for themselves upon discharge. The difficulty and added expense of providing the CMI care explains, in part, the historic unwillingness of the private sector to serve chronic patients. Instead, private hospitals have preferred those patients with uncomplicated diagnoses or few social complications (Abramovitz 1985; Bergstand 1982).

In addition, recent adjustments in reimbursement rates for Medicaid patients have meant that private hospitals frequently view Medicaid patients as financial liabilities (Zukerman 1987). In fact, a study of Medicaid program data from 1977–84 showed:

> [H]ospitals may find Medicaid patients less desirable and may implement procedures geared toward reducing the number of beneficiaries admitted. (Zukerman 1987, p. 75)

Plans to privatize make reference to the fact that private hospitals will incur some bad debt. However, the fact that Medicaid reimbursement for the CMI is generally lower than the cost of care is minimized. Private hospitals are to designate so many psychiatric beds as "proxy beds," for CMI only, in which the state agrees for a limited time to reimburse the private hospital for a percentage of bad debt incurred as the result of serving the CMI. The reimbursement for bad debt assumes that the private hospital will be able to assign most CMI patients to Medicaid. However, missing from the reimbursement assumptions is the fact that Medicaid has a lower reimbursement rate than other third-party payers. The effect on the CMI is obvious: first, in order to make a profit, the private hospital must provide a different level of care to the CMI than to those patients whose care is paid for by third-party payers such as Blue Cross/Blue Shield; and second, the private hospital is likely to discourage admissions, perhaps even refuse them, if the percentage of bad debt incurred in the proxy beds exceeds the reimbursement from the state.

In the State of Maryland, the Mental Health Association has endorsed the plan because they see a chance to redistribute some money from the state hospital system to the community. However, even when populations in state hospitals decline, states have been unwilling to shift funds to the community (Frank 1989). The losers, much like in the 1960s and 1970s, are those CMI who need hospitalization. Thus, the "shell game," in which it is argued that the only way the community programs can be adequately funded is to destroy the state hospital, harms the CMI by providing them with an inadequate state hospital system and a grossly underfunded community system. New leadership is needed, both at the federal and state levels, that recognizes the importance of adequate funding for both the state hospital and the community.

Integration of State Hospital Care

Our focus on the need for hospitalization is not meant to suggest that resources should be shifted from the community to the state hospital. On the contrary, adequate funding for both the community and the state hospital system is necessary in the continuum of care. Despite the troublesome and often cumbersome bureaucracies of state hospitals, the fact remains that it is unlikely that adequate numbers of hospital beds for the CMI will be created in the private sector. As already discussed, the financial incentives needed to encourage the private sector to serve costly, sick, and often troublesome patients will place a heavy financial drain on the economy. In addition, this process does not add to the infrastructure of care for the CMI. Instead, it creates a *temporary* care environment that is dependent on the government's willingness to reimburse the private market.

An alternative approach is to adequately fund state hospitals so appropriate inpatient care to the CMI can be provided. The most obvious obstacle to this approach is the historic reluctance of state officials to accept fiscal responsibility for the CMI. Lynn (1980) observes:

> Elected state officials have on the whole a greater sense of responsibility toward economy and efficiency in governmental operations than they do toward the effectiveness of coverage of human services. A composite view is

"human services have no constituency. Their clients do not vote, at least not in large enough numbers to make a difference to the average legislator. The average voter is concerned about his or her taxes and wants assurances that revenues are not wasted." Even governors who have reputations as being "for" human services, such as Askew and Evans, could not ignore the economy issue, nor could the heads of their human service organizations. (p. 18)

Lynn's summary of the political process in the states in relation to human services highlights the difficulty in extracting more money from elected state officials for state hospitals. It is not that many states do not have adequate financial resources; instead, state officials know that longevity in their jobs depends on their ability to keep taxes to a minimum.

Therefore, an upgraded state hospital system is dependent upon federal dollars because it is unlikely, if not impossible, to expect state governments to raise taxes or divert resources so that their state hospital systems function properly. Conservative politicians have long known that "governments directly accountable to local voters will choose to spend less than a central government where the voters' will is filtered through interest groups" (Peterson 1984, p. 218). President Reagan applied this philosophy with vigor by reducing and eliminating many grant programs to the states. His aim was simple: have local taxpayers determine what programs they would support. The overall effect of Reagan's strategy has been to force states to make hard choices between those programs they want. Support for enhanced mental health services, particularly improved state hospitals, has not been among the programs taxpayers have endorsed. In the end, taxpayers are generally unwilling to support a program unless it directly benefits them.

An alternative to reforming the state hospital system is a system of care in the community, such as case management, that is designed to reduce inpatient days and replace the need for the state hospital.

Alternatives to Hospitalization

Case management through the Community Support Program is currently being used as one means of reducing state hospital census. This program, initiated in 1974 by the National Institute on Mental Health, provides states with grants to upgrade support services for the CMI. Unfortunately, the program has been woefully underfunded. One of the thrusts of the program has been a focus on case management.

A study in Seattle found that a combination of case managers with low caseloads, crisis intervention teams, and emergency housing could reduce the number of hospitalizations for their clients (Dickstein et al. 1988). While it may be promising to reduce the number of hospitalizations, few alternative to hospitalization studies comment on the functioning of the patient. In other words, is staying out of the hospital positive for the patient? The assumption among many is that it is; however, this issue remains controversial. Lamb (1988) sums up one of the major problems with continued efforts that focus on the place of treatment instead of care:

> Where to treat should not be an ideological issue; it is a decision best based on the *clinical* needs of each person. . . . Where mentally ill persons are treated has been seen as more important than how they are treated. (p. 941)

In fact, many of the alternative to hospitalization strategies are driven by cost considerations and not clinical determinants. A recent study examined five years of intensive case management with 72 young recidivistic, treatment-resistant CMI patients (Borland et al. 1989). Its conclusions are not surprising:

> [T]he majority of treatment-resistant, thought-disordered chronic patients can be stabilized outside the hospital over an extended period of time. Such an accomplishment requires individualized, persistent, often frustrating efforts employing a variety of strategies and interventions to provide and maintain *hospital-like* functions in the community. (p. 376)

The study also concludes that intensive case management is equally as expensive as hospital care.

Similar findings were reported by a study in West Germany, also a market-driven economy: "The cost of community care was found to be substantially lower than that of hospital care for less disabled patients, but it *exceeded* the cost of hospital care for the more disabled" (Hafner and Heiden 1989, p. 59).

These two studies highlight a fact that many clinicians know, but mental health policy makers have wanted to ignore: while many CMI can be adequately served in the community, some severely ill people need hospital or hospital-like conditions. This raises the possibility that *good-quality community care* is as expensive, if not more expensive, than state hospital care. In addition, it suggests that more severely ill CMI need a level of care that may not be feasible or possible in the community. Researchers have known that the CMI are not a homogenous population and have a variety of needs. Despite this knowledge, there continues to be much discussion about an alternative to a hospital-based system.

It is particularly important to recognize that alternatives to hospital-based programs that overlook or minimize differences in patients will inevitably fail. This is particularly important to recognize for those patients who need a structured environment. As early as 1979, scholars were aware of patients who were so ill that a nonstructured environment created a stressful situation in which the patients failed to continue their psychotropic medication (Linn et al. 1979). This finding holds true today as well. The human factor of noncompliance is difficult to separate from people who may be so cognitively disorganized or decompensated that they are unable to realize the need to take psychotropic medications.

Instead of matching patient needs with specific programs, alternatives to hospitalization strategies assume that the majority of, if not all, patients benefit from avoiding the hospital. This approach is similar to trying to force square pegs into round holes. Creating a mental health system that can adequately respond to the community as well as inpatient needs of the CMI requires adequate funding for fully developed community and hospital approaches to care.

A Rational Mental Health Policy

As opposed to the poor person who is physically and mentally able to participate in the mainstream economic system, many of the CMI are incapable, because of their illness, of working and being self-sufficient. Consequently, the CMI are dependent upon the government to provide funding for their care. This can be done by providing them with insurance, such as Medicaid, that they can use to purchase care in the traditional medical market system. On the other hand, a separate public system can be maintained for their care.

Medicaid has been a failure in many ways because the needs of patients have continually been sacrificed in order to maintain the cost of the program at a reasonable level. A market system assumes that consumers and providers establish a price that is based on supply and demand. Providers may charge $20, but consumers may decide that price is too high and forgo that purchase. The CMI, in general, cannot forgo medical care because their functioning is often so tenuous that the failure to adjust their medication can result in significant decompensation or toxicity.

Because medical costs for the CMI do not respond to normal market forces, the federal government is placed in the position of either rationing services to the CMI or paying rising medical costs. In our view, neither alternative is helpful to the CMI. The first alternative results in patients being turned away from hospitals or being prematurely discharged. The second alternative consumes needed resources and redistributes them inappropriately to the private sector. As noted throughout this book, such approaches do not develop an infrastructure that can provide ongoing services to the poor.

The most rational approach is to develop and operate a separate mental health system for the CMI. They will not have to compete against unfair odds because their insurance reimbursement is lower, and the system will become part of the permanent infrastructure of the public sector. Most important, this approach recognizes the dependency needs of the CMI. Critics may charge that this separation of the CMI increases their stigma. However, mainstreaming has been a failure, and the dependency needs of the CMI are simply not compatible with America's market-dominated economy. Therefore, we believe it is more humane to recognize the fact that many CMI will remain dependent and not be able to participate in the economic mainstream. The result of these initiatives will be the elimination of homelessness for many of the CMI.

We believe the following recommendations will create a more unified system of care for the CMI: first, switch control of state hospitals to the federal government; second, improve and reform state hospital care; third, upgrade community care by providing consistent funding through a combination of federal and state grants; fourth, change commitment statutes; and finally, fifth, mandate services such as mobile treatment, crisis intervention, and intensive case management.

The shifting of control of the state hospital from state to federal is a dramatic shift in federal-state relations. Nevertheless, it is politically possible because states have long wanted to reduce their financial liability by extricating themselves from direct patient care. The federal government, unlike the states, has a successful history of operating hospitals, as seen in its operation of hospitals for armed services personnel and veterans. Rather than have the federal government funnel money to the states, then create a state bureaucracy to manage the funds, and then be concerned about compliance issues, it is more rational to have the federal government directly manage state hospitals.

A unique way to fund this approach is to have the National Institute of Mental Health (NIMH) use more of its money to pay for direct care. The Community Support Program project used elements of this approach; however, priorities within the Reagan administration shifted the focus away from direct patient care. Nevertheless, NIMH continues to receive federal support, but NIMH monies are now used primarily to fund reaseach. How much research is necessary? Does much of the research duplicate itself? Could some of the research dollars be shifted to direct care and not sacrifice potential insights about future treatments for the CMI? These questions need to be answered before any new budget appropriations are made to fund direct patient care at the federal level.

Reform of the state hospital is also necessary. First, all professionals at the facility would have to meet the licensing requirements of that state. Second, pay would be adjusted to attract and more fairly compensate highly qualified staff. Third, length of patient stay would be determined by clinical judgment and not administrative criteria. Fourth, services, such as psychotherapy, vocational rehabilitation, and art therapy would be implemented as dictated by the needs of the patient. Fifth, step-down facilities would be developed on hospital grounds where patients approaching discharge could more gradually engage the community.

Finally, asylums would be created on hospital grounds for patients who are in need of a structured environment but do not need to be in a hospital.

It is important to locate these asylums on state hospital grounds so that the CMI do not become neglected. Our use of the word *asylum* does not suggest that we want to return to the days when patients were left to live in over-crowded and inhumane institutions. On the contrary, we advocate places of sanctuary where patients who are not able to currently benefit from medica-tion or psychosocial approaches can be provided with safety and adequate food, clothing, and shelter. These would not be places or permanent confine-ment. Instead, patients would be evaluated on a regular basis and placed back in the hospital when their condition improved enough and they could benefit from psychiatric and psychosocial interventions. Eventually, many of these patients could return to the community. However, this return should only take place when the patient is ready and able to live in the community. By keeping asylums on hospital grounds, patients could be moved back to the hospital and the asylums would be able to take advantage of the latest advances discovered by state hospitals.

Once individuals return to the community, quality community care is important to prevent decompensation. Therefore, rather than relying on the current patchwork of funding sources in which patients can easily fall through the cracks, we argue that a system of matching grants should be developed in which the states and the federal government would equally participate. Management of the program would be the state's responsibility, yet our last proposal would mandate that each CMHC provide certain services. This mandate would be linked to federal funding, and states that did not comply would be confronted with the elimination of some federal funds. An addi-tional way to add leverage to this process is for the federal funds in question to be highway funds. This would mean that if a state chose to not adequately fund their mental health program, not only the CMI, but also middle-class taxpayers, would suffer as a result.

Consistent funding is currently one of the major impediments in the care of the CMI. The requirement that states match federal grants enables the fed-eral government to leverage money from states. Much like all of our pro-posals, this approach requires leadership on the federal level to ensure that the federal grants are adequate to meet the needs of the CMI. This goal can be best attained by shifting the focus of NIMH away from research and toward providing quality services for the CMI. A set of mandated services is the approach we recommend.

Mandated services would include those designed to provide patients with continuous care from the moment they leave the hospital through their tenure in the community. If they need to go back to the hospital, commitment laws would be adjusted so they could either admit themselves or they could be com-mitted, even if they were not suicidal or homicidal.

To many, liberals and conservatives alike, the enormous federal deficit is a deterrent to this type of program. However, this assumes that it is inappropriate to fund new programs through new taxes. In chapter 3 we discussed different ways of increasing revenues to the federal government. The most obvious approach is to raise marginal tax rates in a progressive fashion.

These added revenues can create the necessary resources to adequately fund a hospital and community-based program. Will this prevent homelessness? Some of the CMI will continue to decompensate and become homeless; however, an integrated system of care will be better able to prevent decompensation and, when it does occur, quickly provide the resources necessary to hasten recovery.

Our recommendations depend on the willingness of the American people to recognize, first, that the CMI are a dependent population and, second, that their dependency prevents them from being able to participate in the mainstream economy. In many ways, much of the American electorate is willing to recognize that the CMI are different and that they are not able to fully function in society. At the same time, however, the American experience in which some, but not all, have been able to "pull themselves up by their boot straps" makes significant funding changes for the CMI unlikely. John Talbott (1987) observes:

> It is my prediction that given the current political climate, economic trends, and governmental social, mental health, and housing policies, things will get worse for the chronically mentally ill before they get better. I fear that the numbers of the homeless will continue to rise. . . . (p. 26)

Unfortunately, Talbott's prediction is still viable in 1989. The political will to make the system more responsive to the needs of the CMI, even with a less radical program than the one we propose, is not forthcoming on the horizon. Much like any effort to help a disenfranchised group such as the CMI, enlightened leadership at the national level is necessary. However, any increased efforts to help the CMI also will require increased funding. This is the greatest stumbling block that prevents the needs of the CMI from being addressed because, thus far, the American public has been unwilling to adequately underwrite programs for individuals who are unable to survive on their own.

References

Abramovitz, M. (1985). The privatization of the welfare state: A review. *Social Work, 7*, 259.

Andrulis, D.P. & Mazade, N.A. (1983). American mental health policy: Changing directions in the 80s. *Hospital and Community Psychiatry, 3*, (7) 601–11.

Anthony, W.A., Cohen, M., Farkas, M. & Cohen, B.F. (1988). Case management— More than a response to a dysfunctional system. *Community Mental Health Journal, 24*, (3): 219–28.

Appleby, L. & Desai, P. (1985). Documenting the relationship between homelessness and psychiatric hospitalization. *Hospital and Community Psychiatry, 36,* 732–37.

Arce, A.A. & Vergare, M.F. (1984). Identifying and characterizing the mentally ill among the homeless. In Lamb, H.R. (ed.), *The Homeless Mentally Ill.* Washington, D.C.: The American Psychiatric Association.

Bassuk, E.L., Rubin, L. & Lauriat, A. (1984). Is homelessness a mental health problem? *American Journal of Psychiatry, 141,* 1546–49.

Bassuk, E.L. & Gerson, S. (1978). Deinstitutionalization and mental health services. *Scientific American, 238,* 46–53.

Belcher, J.R. (1988a). Are jails replacing the mental health system for the homeless mentally ill? *Community Mental Health Journal, 24,* (3): 185–95.

———. (1988b). Rights versus needs of homeless mentally ill persons. *Social Work, 33,* (5): 398–402.

———. (1988c). The future role of state hospitals. *The Psychiatric Hospital, 19,* (2): 79–83.

———. (In Press (a)). On becoming homeless: A study of chronically mentally ill patients. *Journal of Community Psychology.*

———. (In Press (b)). Privatization and mental health care: A step backward for the chronically mentally ill. *Social Policy.*

Belcher, J.R. & Toomey, B.G. (1988). Relationship between deinstitutionalization model, psychiatric disability, and homelessness. *Health and Social Work, 13,* 145–53.

Bergstand, L.R. (1982). Big profit in private hospitals. *Social Policy, 13,* 49–54.

Bevilacqua, J.J. & Noble, H.H. (1987). Chronic mental illness: A problem in politics. In Menninger, W.W. & Hannah, G. (eds.), *The Chronic Mental Patient II.* Washington, D.C.: The American Psychiatric Press.

Borland, A., McRae, J. & Lycan, C. (1989). Outcomes of five years of continuous intensive case management. *Hospital and Community Psychiatry, 40,* (4): 369–76.

Bostick, M.R., Kirkman, G.M. & Samuel, M.B. (1983). Individual rights versus the therapeutic state: An advocacy model for respondent's counsel in civil commitment. *Capital University Law Review, 13,* 139–74.

Brown, B. (1983). The impact of political and economic changes upon mental health. *American Journal of Orthopsychiatry, 53,* 583–92.

Chu, F. & Trotter, S. (1974). *The Madness Establishment.* New York: Grossman.

Ciompi, L. (1980). Three lectures on schizophrenia: The natural history of schizophrenia in the long-term. *British Journal of Psychiatry, 136,* 413–20.

Dickstein, D., Hanig, D. & Grosskopf, B. (1988). Reducing treatment costs in a community support program. *Hospital and Community Psychiatry, 39,* (10): 1033–35.

Durham, M.L. (1985). Implications of need-for-treatment laws: A study of Washington State's involuntary treatment act. *Hospital and Community Psychiatry, 36,* 975–77.

Foley, H.A. & Sharfstein, S.S. (1983). *Madness and Government: Who Cares for the Mentally Ill?* Washington, D.C.: American Psychiatric Press.

Frank, R.G. (1989). The medically indigent mentally ill: Approaches to financing. *Hospital and Community Psychiatry, 40,* (1): 9–12.

General Accounting Office (1978). *Returning the mentally disabled to the community: Government needs to do more.* Washington, D.C: Government Printing Office.

Goldman, H.H. (1984). Epidemiology. In Talbott, J.A. (ed.), *The Chronic Mental Patient/Five Years Later.* New York: Grune and Stratton, 16.

Grob, G. (1983). *Mental Illness and American Society: 1875 to 1940.* Princeton, N.J.: Princeton University Press.

Gronfein, W. (1985). Psychotropic drugs and the origins of deinstitutionalization. *Social Problems, 32,* 437–54.

Hafner, H. & Heiden, W. (1989). Effectiveness and cost of community care for schizophrenic patients. *Hospital and Community Psychiatry, 40,* (1): 59–63.

Harbin, H.T. & Anderson, M.E. (1988). *Maryland Meets the Challenge: The Public-Private Partnership.* Annapolis, MD: Mental Health Administration.

Harrow, M., Larin-Kettering, I., Prosen, M. & Miller, J.G. (1983). Disordered thinking in schizophrenia: Intermingling and loss of set. *Schizophrenia Bulletin, 9,* 354–67.

Hearings (1955). Subcommittee on Health and Education. Committee on Education and Labor, U.S. Senate.

Hearings (1963). Subcommittee of the Committee on Interstate and Foreign Commerce, House of Representatives. March 26–28.

Lamb, H.R. (1984). The need for continuing asylum and sanctuary. *Hospital and Community Psychiatry, 37,* 798–802.

———. (1988). Deinstitutionalization at the crossroads. *Hospital and Community Psychiatry, 39,* (9): 941–45.

Lamb, H.R. & Grant, R.W. (1982). The mentally ill in an urban county jail. *Archives of General Psychiatry, 39,* 17–22.

Linn, M.W., Caffey, E.W., Klett, J., Hogarty, G.E. & Lamb, H.R. (1979). Day treatment and psychotropic drugs in aftercare. *Archives of General Psychiatry, 36,* 1055–66.

Lynn, L.E. Jr. (1980). *The State and Human Services.* Cambridge, MA: MIT Press.

Morrissey, J.R. & Goldman, H.H. (1984). Cycles of reform in the care of the chronically mentally ill. *Hospital and Community Psychiatry, 35,* 785–93.

Okin, R.L. (1984). Expand the community care system: Deinstitutionalization can work. *Hospital and Community Psychiatry, 36,* 742–45.

Passamanick, B., Scarpitti, F.R. & Dinitz, S. (1967). *Schizophrenics in the Community.* New York: Appleton-Century-Crofts.

Peterson, G.E. (1984). Federalism and the states. In Palmer, J.L. & Sawhill, I.V. (eds.), *The Reagan Record.* Cambridge, MA: Ballinger Publishing Company, 217–59.

Scheff, T.J. (1984). *Being Mentally Ill: A Sociological Theory,* 2nd ed. New York: Aldline Publishing Company.

Sharfstein, S.S. & Clark, H.W. (1978). Economics and the chronic mental patient. *Schizophrenic Bulletin, 4,* 399–414.

Steffan, S. (1985). Right to counsel in civil commitment proceedings. *Mental Physical Disability Law Reporter, 9,* 220–37.

Talbott, J.A. (1987). The chronic mentally ill: What do we know, and why aren't we implementing what we know? In Menninger, W.W. & Hannah, G. (eds.), *The Chronic Mental Patient II.* Washington, D.C.: The American Psychiatric Press.

Teplin, L.A. (1983). The criminalization of the chronically mentally ill: Speculation in search of data. *Psychological Bulletin, 9,* 54–67.

Uhler, S.F. (1986). The constitutional right of the indigent facing involuntary civil commitment to an independent psychiatric examination. *Akron Law Review, 20,* 71–93.

Wanck, B. (1984). Two decades of involuntary hospitalization legislation. *American Journal of Psychiatry, 141,* (1): 33–8.

Zuckerman, S. (1987). Medicaid hospital spending: Effects of reimbursement and utilization control policies. *Health Care Financing Review, 9,* 65–77.

7
Homelessness and Alcohol

Brent B. Benda
Elizabeth D. Hutchison

Homelessness has reached a scale only heretofore matched by the depression years of the 1930s (Redburn & Buss 1986; Rosnow et al. 1985). Although questions about the causes of homelessness and discussion of the increasing prevalence of homelessness are important for governmental policy, it would seem, as Crystal (1984) has suggested, that discussions about the etiology of homelessness are most productive when addressing particular subgroups. This chapter, therefore, will take a more limited focus on alcohol abusers and homelessness.

How is it that even the most conservative estimates indicate that alcohol abuse is three times more common among the homeless than among the general population? Why are alcohol abusers disproportionately represented among the homeless? Whatever explanations we construct must take into account that historical review indicates a stable pattern over the past century in terms of the proportion of alcohol abusers among the homeless population (Stark 1987). The numbers of homeless have varied over the years (Redburn & Buss 1986), but the proportion of alcohol abusers among them has not varied significantly.

Clinicians and researchers have developed a variety of definitions for alcohol abuse, and the different definitions have been demonstrated to produce very different reports about prevalence (Vaillant 1983). Alcohol abuse is usually considered to become alcohol dependence when there is evidence of physical tolerance or physiological withdrawal. For the purposes of this chapter, the term "alcohol abuse" will be used, generally, to describe situations in which alcohol use "has taken on a life of its own" (Vaillant 1983), producing a variety of social problems for the abusing individual. No attempt is made, except in reporting research in which such distinctions are made, to distinguish between alcohol abuse and alcohol dependence.

Brent B. Benda, Ph.D., is an assistant professor at the University of Arkansas/Little Rock. Elizabeth D. Hutchison, Ph.D., is an assistant professor at Virginia Commonwealth University. Contributions to this chapter were equal between the two; their names are listed alphabetically.

Contemporary professional literature on homelessness refers often to the "new homeless" and emphasizes the heterogeneity and interlocking problems that characterize the current homeless population (Crystal 1984; Kaufman 1984; Hagen 1987). This emphasis on heterogeneity, while accurate, has sometimes resulted in an unnecessary and unfortunate de-emphasis on the special needs of the homeless alcohol abuser.

The purpose of the first part of this chapter is to discuss the relationship between alcohol abuse, economic dislocation and homelessness; to present information on alcoholism; and to address current understandings regarding prevalence, demographic characteristics, and origins of the homeless alcohol abuser. The second part of the chapter reports an analysis of alcohol abuse from an exploratory study of homeless people in Richmond, Virginia and discusses policy and practice implications of this and other research.

Economic Dislocation and Housing Issues

The consistent over-representation of alcohol abusers among the homeless suggests a complex interlocking of problems of alcohol abuse, economic dislocation, and homelessness. Rosnow et al., (1985) observes:

> [C]onditions in the job market and . . . conditions in the housing market set the stage for the occurrence of homelessness. Mediating conditions and precipitating events add layers of complexity so that it can be said no two persons become homeless in exactly the same fashion. The most common mediating conditions . . . [are] criminal conviction, a history of mental illness, and a history of alcohol or other drug abuse. Persons with these histories or conditions are especially vulnerable. The most frequently encountered precipitating events [are] loss of a job, loss of support . . . , divorce or separation of spouses, and other conflict among family members or friends. (p. 9)

From this framework, we suggest that there is a relationship between alcohol abuse and economic dislocation, and that the complex interaction of the two increases the likelihood of homelessness.

In addition, a dramatic stage-setting factor involves changes in the housing market (Belcher & Singer 1988). Wittman (1985) suggests that "much of the blame for the presence of homelessness generally, and among people with alcohol problems in particular, may be attributed to declines in the availability of housing for low-income, high problem groups" (p. 6). Rejection from housing has been a long-standing problem for alcohol abusers, and the decrease in the type of housing units most likely to be available to them seriously jeopardizes the ability of the chronic alcohol abuser to compete in the housing market. During the same period in which the decline in housing units occurred, two innovations in delivery of service to subgroups also altered traditional patterns of housing alcohol abusers.

The first of these innovations was the deinstitutionalization of the state psychiatric hospitals discussed in chapter 6. The impact of this phenomenon is well exemplified by the situation in New York State, where the psychiatric hospital census declined from 80,000 to 23,000 between the late 1960s and early 1980s (Crystal 1984). The failure for development of community-based programming to keep pace with the discharged patients is legend by now. Consequently, many discharged psychiatric patients became competitors for the declining stock of low-income housing. The extent to which alcohol abusers, either singularly or dually diagnosed, were among these discharged patients is unknown, but the evidence suggests that the numbers were significant (Roper & Boyer 1987). It is also unclear to what extent previously hospitalized psychiatric patients without proper diagnosis of alcoholism become self-medicated with alcohol upon hitting the streets; some researchers have suggested that this is sometimes the case (Rosnow et al. 1985).

The second innovation was the decriminalization of public drunkenness. Until the 1960s, the justice system was charged with managing public drunkenness and implemented this charge by arresting public inebriates and incarcerating them for brief periods in the "drunk tank" (Sadd & Young 1987). Once a disease model of alcoholism began to gain popularity, however, it no longer seemed appropriate to manage the problem through the criminal justice system. Passage of the Hughes Act (Uniform Alcoholism and Intoxification Treatment Act) in 1971, and creation of the National Institute of Alcohol Abuse and Alcoholism at about the same time, transferred the management of the public inebriate from the criminal justice system to the health care system (Sadd & Young 1987; Shandler & Shipley 1987). The expectation in this transfer was that the health care system had the expertise to intervene in the cycle of alcoholism and would be able to eliminate the "revolving door" cycle of drunk/drunk tank/drunk. As Sadd and Young (1987) have suggested, this policy change succeeded only in relocating the revolving door, and now the cycle is too often drunk/detox./drunk. Unfortunately, transfer of management of alcoholism to the health care system occurred in a climate of increased stringency for admission to general hospitals (Wittman 1985; Sadd 1985).

The shrinking housing stock for people with problems such as alcoholism has contributed to increasing rates of homelessness and to an increase in the numbers, if not proportion, of homeless alcohol abusers. But what makes chronic alcohol abusers vulnerable to becoming homeless?

Chronic Alcoholism as a Mediating Factor

Fischer and Breakey (1987) have suggested that "for the alcoholic, homelessness may result from the downward drift more closely related to the progress of alcoholism than to lifelong disaffiliation or, perhaps, to mental illness" (p. 61). Although it is becoming increasingly clear that there are many homeless people who could be dually diagnosed with alcoholism and another psychiatric disorder, it still appears that the natural life course of alcoholism is sufficient to render severe alcohol abusers in late stages very vulnerable to becoming homeless.

One of the most authoritative works to date on the life course of alcoholism is Vaillant's *Natural History of Alcoholism* (1983). Vaillant's work is based on the study of 660 men over a forty-year period from 1940 to 1980, and a supplementary sample of 100 men from an alcohol treatment program followed over an eight-year period. The larger sample, of 660, includes 456 inner-city boys chosen for study while in junior high school as well as 204 upper-middle-class college students. They were chosen as representatives of their social strata and not because they had already evidenced signs of alcohol abuse. This study represents a major work in the field of alcoholism because it captures the development of drinking patterns over a forty-year period and also follows a treatment population over an eight-year period.

Vaillant concludes that alcoholism is a "chronic relapsing disease" that develops gradually from social drinking to alcohol abuse to alcohol dependence over a three- to fifteen-year period (Vaillant, p. 148). Vaillant's data confirm earlier studies that 2 to 3 percent of active alcohol abusers achieve stable remission per year. Approximately 10 percent achieve stable remission the first time they seek professional assistance. Over the course of their lives, approximately half of all alcohol abusers achieve stable recoveries. Vaillant's data indicate that, for the average alcohol abuser in remission, stable abstinence was achieved only after ten to fifteen years of severe alcohol abuse. Consequently, the rate of alcohol abuse peaks among twenty- to forty-year-olds, but after age forty, the rate of stable remissions exceeds the rate of new cases, and the rate of alcohol abuse in the total sample decreases. Unfortunately, Vaillant's study, because it does not follow past middle age, fails to inform about the extent to which death is responsible for this waning of alcohol abuse in the later years. The existing data are not encouraging in this area, however, indicating that the mortality rate of alcohol abusers is three times that of the general population. Vaillant reminds us that the four major causes of death among men in the United States between the ages of twenty and forty are alcohol-related maladies: cirrhosis, homicide, suicide, and accidents.

Popular literature often refers to the alcoholic personality, suggesting a picture of "a self-centered, immature, dependent, resentful, irresponsible" person, who is predisposed by these personality traits to become alcoholic

(Vaillant, p. 51). Data from Vaillant's longitudinal sample indicate, however, that premorbidly alcohol abusers do not differ from other people in the personality dimensions ascribed to the alcoholic. If they are distinguishable in any way, it is that they tend to be highly active and outgoing as adolescents. The data also indicate, however, that once alcoholic, the respondents in Vaillant's sample develop the personality patterns attributed to the alcoholic personality. This is in keeping with laboratory research that demonstrates that chronic use of alcohol causes subjects to become withdrawn, less self-confident, more anxious, and often more depressed with increased ideas of suicide. The behaviors that accompany these emotional reactions become increasingly disruptive to social relationships over the life course of severe chronic alcoholism. In fact, complaints of others is a criterion for distinguishing alcohol abuse from heavy social drinking.

Vaillant reports that one-fourth of all alcohol abusers in his sample advanced to chronic alcohol dependence with withdrawal symptoms and need for detoxification. This stage is less malleable than earlier stages of abuse, with the only possible outcomes being abstinence, social incapacity, or death. At this point, unfortunately, alcoholism has destroyed the two key elements of any recovery process: ego strengths and social supports. In addition, physical health may be seriously jeopardized. The alcohol abuser is now most vulnerable to an array of precipitating events that can tip the scales and provoke an episode of homelessness. Vaillant reports his data indicate that "active alcoholism is a powerful barrier to membership in the middle class" (p. 205). This finding suggests that the poor social adjustment that results from severe alcoholism leads to a "drifting down" in social class, leading Vaillant to propose that "severe alcoholism causes low social class (p. 140).

Prevalence of Alcohol Abuse Among the Homeless

Using different definitions and different sampling methodologies, recent descriptive studies of homeless populations in various geographic areas have found that 20 to 50 percent of homeless people have alcohol-related problems. A study of the homeless population in Los Angeles, based on a probability sample of sheltered and non-sheltered homeless, reported that 62.9 percent of the sample of 379 had met the criteria for either alcohol abuse or alcohol dependence at some point in their lives; 41 percent had experienced symptoms in the last three years; and almost 33 percent had experienced symptoms of alcohol abuse within the previous year (Koegel & Burnam 1987). Another study of Los Angeles homeless, using cluster sampling to produce comprehensive interviews with 269 homeless men and women, found that 26 percent of the sample could be classified as alcohol abusers and 19 percent could be classified as alcohol dependent, based on information on lifetime experience with alcohol (Roper & Boyer 1987).

A major study of homelessness in Ohio, conducted in 1984, reported that 27 percent of the sample of 979 had ever gone for help for alcohol problems (Roth & Bean 1985). A systematic random sample of intake interviews from Boston's Long Island Shelter found that 32 percent of the 205 sample cases reported drinking daily, and 40 percent reported that they had received treatment for alcohol abuse at some point (Garrett & Schutt 1987). In a study of 237 homeless people in Milwaukee, 24 percent were categorized as having alcohol/drug abuse problems (Rosnow et al. 1985). From a study of shelter residents in Detroit, key informants at shelters estimated that 33 percent of shelter guests were alcoholics, while 20.5 percent of the guests reported drinking daily, and 31 percent reported having been through an alcohol treatment program at some time (Mowbray et al. 1986).

In a study of the physical health problems of homeless people in sixteen cities, including 80,000 encounters with 30,000 homeless clients, health care providers listed 23 percent of the sample as problem drinkers. Based on the finding that the rate of reported alcoholism increased with more health care contacts, the researchers estimate that 40 percent of homeless men and 10 to 20 percent of homeless women are alcohol abusers (Wright et al. 1987).

In a report on research in progress of a random sample of homeless from missions, shelters, and the jail in Baltimore, Fischer and Breakey (1987) found 50 percent of the sample to be definitely alcoholic and 7.4 percent to be possibly alcoholic. A probability sample of mission residents in Eastern Baltimore found a lifetime prevalence for substance abuse/dependence among this subset of the homeless to be approximately 70 percent (Fischer et al. 1984).

It is interesting to note that estimates from these recent studies regarding the magnitude of alcohol-related problems among the homeless are very similar to survey results dating back to the turn of the century. In a review of a century of surveys on homelessness, Stark (1987) found a great deal of consistency over time, with the possible exception of the depression years of the 1930s, in the estimate of the prevalence of alcoholism among the homeless. Citing twenty-three selected studies of the homeless, covering every decade between 1890 and 1980, Stark found an average alcohol abuse rate of 30 to 33 percent.

Two points become clear in a review of both historical and current surveys of the homeless: alcohol abuse is present in a minority, albeit a large minority, of the homeless population; and yet the prevalence of alcohol abuse among the homeless is far higher than among the general population. Vaillant (1983) indicates that, depending on the definition used, between 3 and 10 percent of the population of the United States will suffer from alcoholism at some point in their lives. If we take the high end of this range, 10 percent, and use Stark's average of 30 percent for the homeless population, the prevalence of alcohol abuse among the homeless is at least three times greater than among the general population. This signifies that service provision to the homeless must include alcoholism services, and alcohol abuse services must direct special attention to the problems of the homeless alcohol abuser.

The Homeless Alcohol Abuser

Research over the last four decades, although evidencing some definitional differences and methodological limitations, has begun to paint a consistent and increasingly vivid picture of the ways in which the homeless alcohol abuser is different, as well as similar, to other homeless persons.

Education

No substantial differences in education were found between the alcohol group and the nonalcohol group in the Ohio study (Roth & Bean 1985). In contrast, a Massachusetts study reports lower educational attainment among persons scoring high on an alcohol scale (Human Services Research Institute 1985).

Marital Status

Several studies have found the homeless alcohol abuser more likely to have been married and divorced than other homeless persons (Fischer & Breakey 1987; Human Services Research Institute 1985). In the Ohio study, 45.1 percent of the alcohol abusing homeless had been divorced, compared with 20 percent of the nonabusing homeless. This study also found that only 3.4 percent of the alcohol abusing homeless are currently married, compared with 10.5 percent of other homeless people (Roth & Bean 1985). Koegel and Burnam (1987) found the singularly diagnosed alcoholic homeless to be much less likely to never have been married and much more likely to be either widowed, divorced, or separated than other groups of homeless. The dually diagnosed group was more likely to have never been married than the singularly diagnosed alcohol abusing group.

Military History

Several studies have found a higher percentage of veterans among the alcohol abusing homeless than in the homeless population in general (Roth & Bean 1985; Koegel & Burnam 1987; Fischer & Breakey 1987). This finding is, of course, confounded by the fact that there is a higher percentage of men among homeless alcohol abusers than in the general homeless population.

Criminal History

Research also has consistently found a much higher percentage of the alcohol abusing homeless to have been in prison than the nonalcohol group. The Ohio study found that 86.8 percent of the alcohol group had been in prison, compared with 51.1 percent of the nonalcohol group (Roth & Bean 1985). It is possible that this finding is partially related to the fact that public drunkenness was processed by the criminal justice sector rather than the health/mental health sector prior to the 1970s. Middle-aged alcohol abusers would have been likely, therefore, to have records of arrests for public drunkenness. Fischer and Breakey (1987) found, however, that not only did the alcohol group have more arrests than other groups, they also had more felony convictions and more arrests within the past year of the study. The respondents attributed their arrests to alcohol. A study of homeless in Milwaukee (Rosnow et al. 1985), found that almost one-half of the homeless with alcohol and drug problems had felony offenses—the highest percentage of any group of homeless.

Length of Homelessness

Recent research suggests that alcohol abusing homeless are more prone to chronic homelessness than other groups. Roth and Bean (1985) found the group of homeless with alcohol problems to have been homeless, on the average, twice as long as others in their homeless sample. They also found that the group with alcohol problems was more transient than the nonalcohol group. Koegel and Burnam (1987) found both the singularly diagnosed and the dually diagnosed alcohol abusing homeless to have longer histories of homelessness than other groups. There were no differences between groups for length of current episode of homelessness, but the singularly diagnosed alcohol abusing group reported a larger number of episodes than other groups. Koegel and Burnam report, however, that the singularly diagnosed alcohol group lived on skid row for the first time at a later age than other groups. Although there are often multiple interlocking reasons for homelessness, alcohol abusing homeless individuals are more likely than those without alcohol problems to give alcohol/drug abuse as the first reason for homelessness (Roth & Bean 1985; Fischer & Breakey 1987). Koegel and Burnam (1987) found the singularly diagnosed alcohol group to be less likely than other groups to give lack of job as the reason for first being homeless and more likely to report lack of money, family crisis, or alcohol.

Employment

When employed, homeless alcohol abusers are more likely to hold temporary jobs, while non-abusing homeless people are more likely to hold permanent jobs (Roth & Bean 1985). These findings, however, did not examine the relationship between the state of the economy and how employers responded to employees who abused alcohol. For example, during a recession employers need to lay off workers. Those workers most likely to be laid off are those that are the least productive. Hence, the worker who abuses alcohol might be laid off.

Social Support Network

The weight of evidence suggests that alcohol abusers are more likely than other homeless to have secure support systems in early life, but that these attachments are destroyed over the life course of alcoholism. Research also indicates that chronic alcoholism is more likely to disrupt family relationships than friendship relationships. Roth and Bean (1985) found that although the alcohol and nonalcohol groups of homeless had similar perceptions of their relationships with relatives, the alcohol group reported a longer period of time since last contact. They found no differences between the groups on period of time since contact with friends. Fischer and Breakey (1987) report that social supports may be greater among alcohol abusing homeless than other homeless, but not as great as in the general population.

Physical Health

No finding is as striking, or as sad, as the finding of severe physical health problems among the homeless alcohol abuser. Roth and Bean (1985) found a higher proportion of the alcohol group reporting physical health problems than in the nonalcohol group. Wright and associates (1987) found in their study of 30,000 homeless people that rates for almost every physical disorder were higher among the alcohol abusing homeless than among the nonabusers. They found alcohol abusers to be

> . . . four to seven times as likely to suffer from liver disease, twice as likely to suffer serious traumas, two to three times as likely to be disabled by seizure disorders or other neurological impairments, and also twice as likely to present with various nutritional deficiencies. . . . Other disorders that are at least 50 percent more common among the alcohol abusers than among the others include hypertension, chronic obstructive pulmonary disease, gastrointestinal disorders, and arterial disease. (p. 24–5)

Fischer and Breakey (1987) found more traumatic injury among the alcohol abusing homeless than among other groups.

Mental Health

The research findings also indicate a strong correlation between alcohol abuse and mental health problems in the homeless population. In the Ohio study (Roth & Bean 1985), only minor differences existed between the alcohol and nonalcohol groups of homeless in self-reports of mental health status, although the alcohol group was much more likely to report that their life had been "not very satisfying." Performance on the Psychiatric Severity Index, however, found the alcohol group to be more dysfunctional—particularly on scales for depression-anxiety and suspicion-persecution-hallucination. There were no differences between the groups for behavioral disturbance severity.

Wright and associates (1987) found mental illness to be significantly more likely among alcohol abusers than among nonabusers. Alcohol abusers were also more likely to be engaged in drug abuse than nonabusers. In a study of dually diagnosed (alcohol plus other psychiatric disorders) homeless people, Koegel and Burnam (1987) found that antisocial personality and drug abuse or dependence were more common among alcohol abusers than among homeless people with other psychiatric disorders. They also found that ". . . those with alcohol diagnoses had a greater number of additional diagnoses than those with no alcohol diagnosis" (p. 30). Not surprisingly, given these findings, Koegel and Burnam found that alcohol abusing homeless were more likely to be experiencing current psychological distress. Fischer and Breakey (1987) found alcohol abusing homeless more likely than other groups of homeless to report recent symptoms of general distress and to report personal and family histories of psychiatric treatment. They did not find evidence of increased cognitive impairment among the alcohol abusing group, however.

Family History

Findings about family history of alcohol abuse among the homeless alcohol abuser mirrors the distribution of alcohol abuse in the population at large. Fischer and Breakey (1987), in their preliminary findings in Baltimore, report that alcohol abusing homeless are three times as likely as nonabusing homeless to report that one or both parents had a drinking problem, and approximately four times as likely to report that one or more siblings had a drinking problem.

A Study of Alcohol Abuse Among the Homeless

Given the apparent evolving patterns of dysfunction presented by many homeless people who abuse alcohol, we decided to examine alcohol abuse among the homeless from a "drift-down" theoretical perspective (Kessler & Cleary 1980). The drift-down perspective hypothesizes that continuing deviance, in this case alcohol abuse, lead to personal and social deterioration, and eventual dysfunction (Vaillant 1983), which can result in homelessness. At the same time, as Vaillant observes, the events, processes, and sequences entailed in the drift-down path of alcoholism are not as yet fully specified.

Without attempting to enter the debate about whether alcoholism is a disease or the result of personality characteristics, the assumption underlying this hypothesis is that people who become addicted to alcohol tend to exhibit a lifelong pattern of problems (see Vaillant 1983; Robins 1974; and Wootton 1959). In part, because the various subgroups within the homeless population have not been delineated in research, there is a paucity of theory and policy directions for intervention. The purpose of the following study is twofold: to examine bivariate relationships to alcoholism among homeless people such as gender and criminal behavior, since there are neglected factors in the literature (Benda, in press; Benda & Dattalo 1988 and 1989); and to test predictions derived from a drift-down theoretical perspective.

Subjects

There were 444 (313 men) homeless people interviewed in Richmond, Virginia during the study period of nineteen months. This period of study eliminated the seasonal sampling bias seen in most research on homeless people. Typically, studies on homelessness consist of small samples selected during a brief period from a shelter or meal program. Since this study was designed to investigate personal characteristics and level of problems, every effort within a limited budget was made to ensure a representative sample of Richmond's population. Using monthly lists of individuals who were contacted by the two major providers of services to the homeless, systematic random samples (Smith, 1981) were drawn each month, with equivalent numbers of respondents interviewed each of the nineteen months.

One agency was the only drop-in counseling center, which also housed the largest meal program in the city, medical services, and all major social services to the homeless. The other agency was the local mental health center, which dispatched a "street team" that went throughout the city to make crisis interventions and referrals. This team purposefully looked for homeless people who were in trouble but not likely to seek out services on their own. These two agencies appeared, from practice experience, to contact the vast majority of, if not all, homeless persons who remained in the city for more than a few days. The sample was defined and described in prior publications (e.g., Benda 1987).

Data Collection

Data were collected through interviews (n = 344) done by eleven graduate social work students and (n = 100) four social workers, who comprised a street team that provided services to homeless people from the city mental health center. These interviewers were given training of twelve two-hour sessions in interviewing and the use of the questionnaire, a one hundred-item instrument (see Benda 1986).

The survey instrument was informed by literature, practice experience, and the use of a panel of homeless people and professionals who work with them. It was pilot-tested with ten homeless people prior to the study, and revisions were made accordingly. The questionnaire took from one-half hour to one and a half hours to administer, depending on the loquacity of respondent. Due to the engagement skills of interviewers and the willingness of homeless people to talk about their problems, the refusal rate was about 5 percent. In addition to the items used in the following analyses, there were questions about work history, benefits applied for and received, needs, medical problems, and family history.

In this study, alcohol abusers were defined with two criteria: if they had been in an alcohol treatment program; and if they currently drink at least a six-pack of beer or four drinks five or more days monthly. This latter criterion is most frequently used in the literature (Vaillant, 1983).

Bivariate Results

Tables 7–1 and 7–2 display the statistically significant (alpha = 0.05) bivariate relationships regarding whether or not individuals in the sample were ever treated for alcohol abuse. Categorical variables also tested included employment (some work/no work), income ($180 or less monthly/more income), living situation (street/other), psychiatric hospitalization (none/some), and source of income (salary-benefits/other). Among the statistically significant factors, shown in table 7–1, we note that a greater percentage of males (27 percent) than females (16 percent) have been in alcohol treatment. Also, more whites (28 percent) than minorities (20 percent), and less singles (20 percent) than married or separated and divorced people (29 percent) have been in alcohol treatment. In the total sample 23 percent have been alcohol treatment.

Other findings of particular note are that a greater percentage of former prisoners (33 percent) than others in the sample (21 percent) have been treated for alcohol abuse. Sadly, we also observe that a higher percentage of those who presently drink at least a six-pack of beer or four drinks five or more days a month (27 percent) are former participants in alcohol treatment than those (17 percent) who drink less. More of those who presently hallucinate (39 percent) have been in alcohol treatment than other homeless (19 percent) in the study.

Table 7–2 presents statistically significant bivariates measured at interval or ratio levels. Irrelevant factors also tested included education, weeks lived in Richmond, siblings, age of first arrest, current arrests, age first used other drugs, and imprisonments. People who have been in alcohol treatment, on

Table 7–1
Factors Related to Whether or Not Homeless Persons Ever Have Been in Alcohol Treatment

Factor	Alcohol Treatment	No Alcohol Treatment	Chi Square	p Value	Phi
Gender					
Male	229	84			
	73%	27%	5.39	.020	.12
Female	110	21			
	84%	16%			
Race					
White	161	64			
	72%	28%	4.48	.035	.11
Minority	178	43			
	81%	20%			
Marital Status					
Single	188	49			
	80%	20%	4.74	.030	.09
Other	141	58			
	71%	29%			
Imprisonment					
No	271	74			
	79%	21%	4.80	.030	.09
Yes	68	33			
	67%	33%			
Current drinking					
Less than five	104	21			
	83%	17%	4.39	.035	.11
Five or more	235	86			
	73%	27%			
Hallucinations					
No	276	67			
	81%	19%	15.14	.000	.19
Yes	63	40			
	61%	39%			
Veteran					
Yes	67	41			
	62%	38%	15.59	.000	.20
No	268	62			
	81%	19%			
Services					
No	259	71			
	79%	21%	3.76	.053	.10
Yes	80	36			
	69%	31%			

Note: "Current drinking" is number of days each month persons drink at least a six-pack or four drinks; "services" are professional contacts monthly.

Table 7–2
More Factors Related to Whether or Not Homeless Persons Ever Have Been in Alcohol Treatment

Factor	Mean	t Value	One-Tailed Probability
Age			
Yes (alcohol treatment)	37.4	2.47	.007
No (alcohol treatment)	33.9		
Children			
Yes	1.55	2.36	.010
No	1.13		
Age first drink			
Yes	14.45	– 3.54	.000
No	16.37		
Juvenile justice			
Yes	0.88	1.77	.039
No	0.39		
Psychiatric hospitalization			
Yes	1.25	1.92	.028
No	0.78		
Other drug hospitalizations			
Yes	0.68	5.34	.000
No	0.12		
Suicide attempts			
Yes	0.86	2.36	.009
No	0.43		
Current drinking			
Yes	9.55	7.07	.000
No	3.14		
Current hallucinations			
Yes	1.05	3.25	.000
No	0.46		
Current other drug use			
Yes	3.34	1.93	.027
No	1.88		
Current victimizations			
Yes	1.56	4.41	.000
No	0.81		

Note: "Juvenile justice" is the number of placements in correctional programs; "current drinking" is number of days each month persons drink at least a six-pack of beer or four drinks; "current hallucinations" are the number weekly; "other drug use" refers to number of days persons use "street drugs" monthly; "victimizations" are the number of times robbed or assaulted in the past year.

the average, are older (37 years of age) than peers (34 years of age) on the street, and they have more children (1.55 versus 1.13). They also began to drink alcohol at an earlier age (14.5 versus 16.4), and have been in more juvenile justice placements. In adulthood, former alcohol program participants report more psychiatric hospitalizations, other drug treatment programs, and suicide attempts than others in the sample. As predicted, these former participants also revealed more current affliction than homeless individuals who have not been treated for alcohol abuse. Former alcohol program participants, for example, presently drink at least a six-pack of beer or four drinks on an average of 9.55 days per month, compared with 3.14 days per month for other homeless people in the sample. They also use nonprescription drugs more days every month (3.34 versus 1.88), and report more victimizations (1.56 versus 0.81) on the streets in the past year.

These figures do not argue well for the effectiveness of several social treatments, and this will be discussed after presenting the multivariate analysis. As hypothesized, tables 7–1 and 7–2 show considerable support for the drift-down perspective. Data indicate that alcohol abuse, crime, and psychiatric problems are interrelated. Alcohol abusers, on the average, began to drink at an earlier age, experienced more juvenile justice placements, had more psychiatric and other drug hospitalizations, and attempted suicide more often than their homeless peers. The former clearly exhibit more current affliction than the latter. Also, a greater percentage of these alcoholics have been in prison than others in the study.

Multivariate Results

To obtain a predictive model of current drinking problems, the regular (ordinary least squares) stepwise regression procedures (Wonnacott & Wonnacott 1970) were employed to examine predictors of the number of days per month people drank at least a six-pack of beer or four drinks. This is the typical level of drinking used to indicate problems (Vaillant 1983). Forty-nine percent of the sample report never drinking this amount, while 24 percent say they drink this amount five or more days per month. Prior to the regression analyses, intercorrelations and scatter plots were checked according to the assumptions of linear regression procedures. Candidate regressors were selected based upon theory and relevant demographics, and included: 1) age; 2) gender; 3) education; 4) employment (work/no work); 5) age first drank; 6) age first used other drugs; 7) age first arrested; 8) juvenile justice placements; 9) psychiatric hospitalizations; 10) imprisonments; and 11) number of alcohol treatment programs.

The statistically significant (alpha = 0.05) predictors of level of present drinking are displayed in table 7–3. In order of predictiveness, the strongest predictor of level of current drinking is the number of alcohol treatment pro-

Table 7–3
Predictors of Current Drinking: Stepwise Regression Procedures

Predictor	B	Beta	t Value	p	R^2 Change
Number of Alcohol treatments	0.761	0.199	3.82	.000	.08
Age of first arrest	− 0.344	− 0.211	− 2.63	.010	.04
Gender	− 5.22	− 0.180	− 2.27	.025	.02
Number of psychiatric hospitalizations	− 0.625	− 0.178	− 2.16	0.33	.03
(Constant)		19.72		5.28	.000

Multiple R = .432   F = 7.40   p = .000 R^2 = .187

Note: B is the unstandarized regression coefficient, whereas Beta is the standardized.

The table shows the current drinking of drinking of homeless persons, which is the number of days each month they drink at least a six-pack of beer or 4 drinks.

grams people have attended in the past, followed by age of first arrest, gender, and number of psychiatric hospitalizations. The positive and negative coefficients demonstrate that current drinking increases as prior alcohol treatment programs increase, as age of first arrest decreases, as psychiatric hospitalizations decrease, and when we consider men as opposed to women. It should be noted that the number of alcohol treatments refers to the number of separate interventions (referrals) or programs, and not to separate office visits or therapy sessions.

The finding that current drinking level increases with a decrease in psychiatric admissions might be surprising, especially in view of the fact that former alcohol treatment participants, on the average, have a greater number of these admissions than others in the sample (see table 7–2). This anomaly is explained by the observation that half of the former psychiatric patients in the sample are within one year of their last release from the hospital. Hence, most of these former patients are still on medications and living in situations that inhibit drinking.

As predicted from the drift-down perspective, the strongest predictor of current level of drinking is prior history of alcohol abuse. Also, an early indicator, crime, predicts present drinking. At the same time, other factors, such as mental illness, are not significant predictors of current drinking once other factors have entered the regression equation, and the significant predictors account for 19 percent (r^2) of the total variance in drinking.

Discussion

Data revealed that 23 percent of the sample (27 percent of the men and 16 percent of the women) have been treated at some time in their lives for alcohol abuse. Further, 24 percent of these people reported that they drank at least a six-pack of beer or four drinks five or more days montly. These figures compare with an estimated 3 to 10 percent of alcoholics in the general population (Vaillant 1983). Hence, the proportion of homeless people who have alcohol problems in this sample is significantly higher than the proportion in the general population.

In certain categories (i.e., men, whites, married or separated/divorced, and former prisoners), the percentages of people who have been in alcohol treatment are each approximately 30 percent. For other categories (i.e., veterans and those who hallucinate), the percentages of former clients of alcohol treatment rise to nearly 40 percent.

Data also show support for the drift-down perspective undergirding the study. Homeless people who have been in alcohol treatment began drinking at an earlier age, were in more juvenile justice placements, had more psychiatric and other drug hospitalizations, and have attempted suicide more often than others in the sample. Moreover, in regard to current affliction, former alcohol program participants report more current drinking, hallucinations, other drug use, and victimizations than others in the study. These findings reveal that a significant proportion of the respondents have ended up homeless after drinking down a path in which crime, alcohol abuse, and psychiatric problems acted together.

There is considerable overlap among people who abuse alcohol, who engage in criminal activity, and who are hospitalized for psychiatric problems. Thirty-three (33 percent) of the 101 persons who have been imprisoned also have been in alcohol treatment, while 40 (30 percent) of the 134 individuals who have been psychiatrically hospitalized have been in therapy for abusing alcohol. This study's data indicate that, for many, these problems began in adolescence and have continued into adulthood. In addition to supporting a general drift-down hypothesis, these results attest to the failure of societal treatments to noticeably alleviate or ameliorate serious problems among these respondents. The bottom line in measuring effectiveness of social interventions is their effect on recidivism, and a significant proportion of these homeless presently are hallucinating and drinking heavily after being in justice, psychiatric, and drug programs since adolescence. These are the chronic mentally ill, habitual drug abusers, and career criminals for whom there are no easy solutions (Blumstein et al. 1986).

The individuals portrayed in this study have no place to call home as a result of multifarious combinations of personal problems, deinstitutionalization policies, and job and housing shortages. While this study only focuses on personal pathology, other research shows that external factors also are responsible for homelessness (Bachrach 1984). Cities are undergoing revitalization of downtown areas and gentrification of urban neighborhoods. While the aesthetic and economic advantages of revitalization are welcome, the negative effect is that the poor are being excluded from the housing market. Single-room occupancy hotels are closing in many cities and being torn down to make room for high-rent office buildings. The decline of low-income housing is occurring simultaneously with the dismantling of federal housing programs.

Inflation, high unemployment, and a decline in availability of unskilled jobs also contribute to homelessness. Homelessness, in large measure, represents an interaction between the most vulnerable in our society and the unequal distribution of resources for the masses. Some are vulnerable and homeless as a direct result of their own behaviors; others are on the street because of deinstitutionalization policies and changes in employment patterns. There are those who have lost jobs and housing due to alcoholism, and those who failed in educational and occupational pursuits because of early drug abuse and crime. These interactive effects leading to homelessness too often are overlooked in the literature and in policy-making arenas (Redburn & Buss 1986). In short, intervention with homeless people, including alcoholics, generally will require a multitudinous approach. Singular interventions may have some potential for amelioration, but too often they are debilitative in practice. For example, providing only shelter for the mentally ill or substance abuser has created dangerous environments, where, incidentally, many homeless refuse to spend a night. Without personal rehabilitation, teaching job skills to an alcoholic is of little avail. In this final section, we present a discussion of policy implications of the study.

Policy and Practice Implications

As with any study, the policy and practice implications of this one are limited by the data analyzed. However, these data clearly reveal that many homeless people are suffering on the streets after several societal interventions since adolescence. Many former alcohol treatment program participants presently are drinking heavily, using other substances, and being victimized on the streets where they now reside. Hence, the echinated question, "What can be done for the homeless alcoholic?"

A long-range, and nonspecific solution to homelessness is prevention. This study reveals that for many homeless people long-term problems, such as alcohol abuse or chronic mental illness, preceded homelessness. Clinical experience suggests that many become homeless after familial support ceased because of their crime and substance abuse. Others appear to be without permanent shelter as a result of mental, learned, or drug-induced intrapsychic frailties. There also are youthful runaways and people (especially women) escaping abusive affiliations who often end up abusing drugs. In short, homelessness, like all hard-core problems, requires prevention as part of the ultimate solution. Until effective intervention strategies are devised to deal with such problems as, for example, incest and sexual abuse of children, there will be unsheltered people who ran away from home. The need for more effective drug prevention programs is highlighted by the findings of this study, and certainly economic dislocation factors need to be addressed.

In terms of more immediate and concrete recommendations for intervention, we need to admit that current deinstitutionalization policies and practices have failed (see Bachrach 1980, 1983; Lamb 1984). With plenteous resources, perhaps the ideas of normalization and community treatment are good; the fact is they have not actually been implemented or tested. The meager facilities (e.g., adult homes) and services (e.g., street teams, drop-in centers) available to the deinstitutionalized are woefully inadequate and undesirable, and according to most measures, promote further dysfunction (Bachrach 1980). Adult homes for offenders and the chronically mentally ill, for example, typically are populated with people with a wide range of pathologies, and this diversity promotes dangerous fears and behavior. Consequently, many mentally ill people actually prefer the streets or returning to a state mental hospital to living in these adult homes. Ironically, many homeless drift across the country in pursuit of asylum, a concept that originally undergirded the creation of the very institutions from which these people are now "liberated" (Lamb 1982; Rothman 1971). The young mentally ill and drug abusers comprise most of these drifters, and they often are unable to be admitted to psychiatric hospitals due to overly stringent admission criteria (Lamb 1984). We believe criteria should be changed to allow admission of people who cannot adjust in the community given current resources.

The fact is that many of the respondents interviewed in this study, who are suffering multiple afflictions, are not being treated. While it has been argued that homeless people rely on informal social systems, and that those informal social systems are better service providers than professionals who are not homeless, these arguments are made by scholars who have not experienced the lack of support these networks, if in existence at all, actually render, or the exploitive nature of many social arrangements on the streets. Many women in the study, for instance, are using nonprescription drugs and/or alcohol, living in abandoned buildings with alcoholic men for intermittent emotional support and security, and suffering the indignities of physical abuse.

The extreme diversity in the problems presented by homeless people, when coupled with their varied symptoms and functional levels, creates a need for highly diversified programs. Since many of these people shun, or are shunned by, traditional service agencies (Bachrach 1984), these services should be centrally located and provided by professionals specially trained to work with homeless individuals. Furthermore, since it is not feasible to locate a comprehensive array of services needed by the homeless in one facility, a solution is to have professionals be available at drop-in centers. These professionals should have the expertise and skill to diagnose clients and make the initial engagement in an informal atmosphere, allowing a bridge to be made to a home agency where longer-term treatment can occur. This recommendation is, in concept, like the one that led to the creation of current drop-in centers for homeless people. However, if the idea is to be effectively implemented, certain key elements must be ensured, or the present ambiguity of services will continue to be ineffectively administered. A major key to this concept of community treatment is having professionals consistently available in these centers—too many of these centers currently are simply gathering places for the homeless and offer no actual services.

Experience indicates that professionals who work with homeless people, especially alcoholics, also must be able to express warmth, a nonjudgmental attitude, and compassion toward perople who often are offensive in hygiene, appreance, and demeanor. At the same time, these professionals need to be able to treat clients informally while holding them accountable for lawless and/or drunken behavior and for some norms of decorum. In other words, professionals who work with these clients must possess a rather rare set of motivations and attributes. Given the multiple problems exhibited by many homeless people in this study, professionals will need to possess considerable diagnostic ability.

Services need to be available to the homeless population in informal drop-in centers, not only to attract people who shun traditional agencies, but also to ensure some comprehensiveness and coordination. Unless comprehensiveness and coordination are deliberately structured into the center's program, experience indicates they do not naturally evolve. Case managers are necessary to ensure that clients are receiving needed services. Also, team meetings concerning individual clients need to occur to develop clear treatment plans that can be monitored (Hagan & Hutchison 1988; Segal and Baumohl 1980; Segal et al. 1977).

As shown in this study, many of the homeless suffer alcohol problems; hence, the proposed center must be closely affiliated with alcohol treatment programs and psychiatric hospitals, and have staff who know these services well. Also, medical complications can result from falls, such as subdural hematomas and fractures, the consequences of exposure such as frostbite or sunburn, and suppression of immune mechanisms that predispose to infection. Clearly, staff in these centers should be familiar with and able to at least begin treatment for alcohol withdrawal syndrome and delirium tremens, which means some immediate access to a physician. Moreover, alcohol consumers on the street frequently use various combinations of drugs, which can induce serious paranoia and psychosis. Irreversible memory deficit, known as Korsakoff's psychosis or alcohol amnestic syndrome, which often follows an acute episode of Wernicke's encephalopathy, a neurological disease, is displayed by several alcoholics on the street. A predisposing factor of Wernicke's encephalopathy and alcohol amnestic syndrome is malnutrition, and this needs to be taken into account in treating street alcoholics. Marchiafava-Bignami disease is another disorder associated with alcoholism in which there is a degeneration of corpus callosum, which is manifested by severe mental dysfunction. Staff in centers for the homeless must be able at least to recognize these pathologies so referrals can be made to appropriate services. These drop-in centers also can serve as place for therapeutic and supportive groups.

Too often, as this study's data show, criminal acts follow heavy drinking bouts. To bring an end to the various destructive behaviors exhibited by a substantial number of homeless individuals and to prevent the syndromes that result from continued heavy drinking, many homeless people must be persuaded to enter detoxification programs and be given the follow-up treatment necessary to ensure some chance of recovery. Only after people have reached a reasonable level of recovery can they be expected to benefit from programs like job training. Research on indigent alcohol abusers demonstrates that most public inebriates leave detoxification units without referral for treatment and without other follow-up plans. And yet, Vaillant (1983) posits that "follow-up is just as essential in the disease called alcoholism as it is in any chronic illness" (p. 305). Recommendations for comprehensive policy for the general homeless population seem well-suited to the subgroup of alcohol abusers. These recommendations suggest the need for a three-tiered continuum of services that includes emergency services, transitional services, and stabilization services. Kaufman (1984) advises that case management must provide the linkages between tiers. Although there appear to be few long-term successes, Sadd (1985) finds that clients have the best follow-up in rehabilitation services if they are allowed to remain in the detoxification facility until an opening is available in a transition facility.

A closer look at the alcohol service system suggests that the problem goes beyond fragmentation and lack of case management and that services in the transitional and stabilization tiers are seriously underdeveloped. More alcohol-free residences are needed for homeless people at various stages of recovery. Long-term residential programs for recovering alcoholics are needed. We also must face the reality of the need to "supply minimum nonpunitive shelter to the actively drinking client" (Vaillant 1983, p. 300). The reluctance to shelter the actively drinking person may explain the finding by Kline and associates (1987) that some alcohol abusing homeless people use detoxification units as a resource to obtain room and board. Wittman (1985) suggests that "[l]ow-income people with special housing needs, such as those with alcohol problems, require special support to compete for housing access" (p. 31). Housing options must be expanded to provide access to people at all stages of the life course of alcoholism.

The data are not encouraging on the efficacy of current treatment technology. Vaillant (1983) concludes, after careful study of his longitudinal data, that clinical treatment does not improve on the natural recovery rate of alcoholism. Given the likelihood that homelessness initially occurs among some individuals with the most intractable of conditions, as well as the possibility that the homeless state exacerbates the abusive condition, it is little wonder that social scientists sound a pessimistic note about the possibilities of positive outcomes for the homeless alcohol abuser (Sadd 1985; Wright et al. 1987).

Service providers must be cognizant of the limitations of current treatment technology, but they should avoid the self-fulfilling prophesy that chronic alcohol abusers cannot be helped. Data are clear that alcoholism does severe damage to the emotional, physical, spiritual, and social well-being of participants and their families, and such pain cannot be ignored. Vaillant (1983) suggests that although remission and relapse remain a mystery for the most part, we should develop the same attitude toward assisting the alcohol abuser that we use with other chronic diseases. Even when we cannot cure, we can provide the care that has the possibility of amelioration (Shandler & Shipley 1987).

When alcoholism became a "disease" rather than a form of deviance, it began to be viewed as another "mental illness." This naturally raised the possibility of involuntary commitment to treatment programs, which had long been an option in service provision for mental illness. The issue of involuntary service to alcohol abusers has strong proponents on both sides of the issue. On the one hand, clinicians argue that pervasive denial systems are a central trait of advanced alcoholism, and that services may have to be imposed to break through these defenses. Some also argue that late-stage alcoholics are a danger to themselves, and sometimes to others, and that danger warrants coercive intervention. Libertarians, on the other hand, argue that involuntary service provision is unconstitutional without due process.

Efforts to develop involuntary services for the protection of homeless people were operationalized by several cities that instituted involuntary sheltering of homeless individuals when the temperature dropped to a certain point during the winter of 1985–86 (Shandler & Shipley 1987). At about the same time, the city of Portland, Oregon began attempts to develop a program of involuntary commitment of late-stage alcoholics who refuse help so that no one would die of alcoholism on the streets. However, this recommendation by the task force met strong opposition when proposed (Newton & Duffy 1987).

The argument about involuntary services for alcohol abusers occurs in a broader context of debate about coercive services. The debate derives from competing societal values for individual freedom on the one hand and for services to the vulnerable on the other. Because both set of values are held dear in this society, the question of whether to mandate services for homeless alcohol abusers, as well as other homeless groups, is not likely to disappear soon.

A final recommendation that is particularly suited to alcoholics who have detoxified is to have publicly financed employment projects where these people can regain their dignity. As already noted in early chapters, this nation's infrastructure is in drastic need of being restored. In addition to providing employment, these projects provide socialization and meaningful activity for people who desperately need both after withdrawing from alcohol and other drugs.

In summary, services to the homeless population currently are woefully insufficient and inadequate. Meager budgets, and thereby limited and under-trained staff, largely are the sources of the deficient response to the social problem of homelessness that characterizes the present care-giving system in this country. These deficiencies lead to other problems, such as vague and uncoordinated services, poor assessments, inconsistent intervention, and lack of follow-through with referrals. Multiple and long-term interventions are nonexistent. The solution to the homeless will be more expensive than current efforts. Trained professionals must be consistently available to those who suffer on the streets, and these staff must be able to diagnose and treat the problems exhibited by a large number of homeless people. Services, in many cases, will have to be plural, and thus well-coordinated. A clear system of account-ability should be instituted to monitor the services. If we do not mount some degree of the recommended efforts, we will witness a permanancy of high levels of homelessness.

References

Bachrach, L.L. (1980). Overview: Model programs for the chronic mental patients. *American Journal of Psychiatry, 137,* 1023–31.

———. (1983). Evaluating the consequences of deinstitutionalization. *Hospital & Community Psychiatry, 34,* 105.

———. (1984). The homeless mentally ill and mental health service: An analytic review of the literature. In Lamb, H.R. (ed), *The Homeless Mentally Ill.* Washington, D.C.: American Psychiatric Association, 11–53.

Belcher, J.R. & Singer, J. (1988). Homelessness: A cost of capitalism. *Journal of Social Policy, 18,* 44–8.

Benda, B.B. (1986). The homeless of Richmond: A report. Unpublished report, Washington, D.C.: National Institute of Mental Health.

———. (1987). Crime, drug abuse, mental illness and homelessness. *Deviant Behavior, 8,* 367–75.

———. (In Press). Crime, drug abuse and mental illness: A comparison of homeless males and females. *Journal of Social Service Research.*

Benda, B.B. & Dattola, P. (1988). Homelessness: Consequence of a crisis or a long-term process? *Hospital and Community Psychiatry, 39,* 884–6.

———. (1989). *Homeless Men and Women: A Study of Problems and Utilization.* Unpublished manuscript.

Blumstein, A., Cohen, J., Roth, J.A. & Visher, C., (eds.) (1986). *Criminal careers and career criminals.* Washington, D.C.: National Academy Press.

Crystal, S. (1984). Homeless men and homeless women: The gender gap. *Urban and Social Change Review, 17,* 2–6.

Fischer, P.J. & Breakey, W.R. (1987). Profile of the Baltimore homeless with alcohol problems. *Alcohol Health & Research World. 11,* 36–7, 61.

Fischer, P.J., Shapiro, B.S., Breakey, W.R., Anthony, J.C. & Kramer, M. (November 1984). *Mental health and social characteristics of the homeless: A survey of mission users.* Paper presented at 112th Annual Meeting of the American Public Health Association, Anaheim, CA.

Garrett, G.R. & Schutt, R.K. (1987). Social services for homeless alcoholics: Assessment and response. *Alcohol Health & Research World. 11,* 50–3.

Hagen, J.L. (1987). Gender and homelessness. *Social Work, 32,* 312–16.

Hagen, J.L. & Hutchison, E. (1988). Who's serving the homeless? *Social Casework, 69,* 491–7.

Human Services Research Institute (1985). *Homelessness Needs Assessment Study: Findings and Recommendations for the Massachusetts Department of Mental Health.* Prepared for Massachusetts Department of Mental Health. Boston, MA: Human Services Research Institute.

Kaufman, N.K. (1984). Homelessness: A comprehensive policy approach. *Urban and Social Change Review, 17,* 21–6.

Kessler, R.C. & Cleary, P.D. (1980). Social class and psychological distress. *American Sociological Review, 45,* 463–78.

Kline, M.V., Bacon, J.D., Chinkin, M. & Manov, W.F. (1987). The client tracking system: A tool for studying the homeless. *Alcohol Health & Research World, 11,* 66–7, 91.

Koegel, P. & Burnam, M.A. (1987). Traditional and nontraditional homeless alcoholics. *Alcohol Health & Research World, 11,* 28–34.

Lamb, H.R. (1982). Young adult chronic patient: The new drifters. *Hospital & Community Psychiatry, 33,* 465–68.

———. (1984). Deinstitutionalization and the mentally ill. *Hospital & Community Psychiatry, 35,* 889–907.

Mowbray, C.T., Johnson, V.S., Solarz, A. & Combs, C.J. (1986). *Mental health and homeless in Detroit: A research study* (NIMH Grant No. 5H84–MH35823–04Sl). Detroit: Michigan Department of Mental Health.

Newton, S.P. & Duffy, C.P. (1987). Old town Portland and an oldtime problem. *Alcohol Health & Research World. 11,* 62–4, 91.

Redburn, F.S. & Buss, T.F. (1986). *Responding to America's Homeless,* New York: Praeger.

Robins, L.N. (1974). *Deviant Children Grown Up: A Sociological and Psychiatric Study of Sociopathic Personality,* reprint. Hunting, NY: Robert E. Krieger.

Roper, F.H. & Boyer, R. (1987). Homelessness as a health risk. *Alcohol Health & Research World. 11,* 38–41, 89.

Rosnow, M.J., Shaw, T. & Concord, C.S. (April 1985). Listening to the homeless: A study of homeless mentally ill persons in Milwaukee (NIMH Grant No. H84MH36388-02S1SRC). Milwaukee: Human Services Triangle, Inc.

Roth, D. & Bean, J. (1985). Alcohol problems and homelessness: Findings from the Ohio study. In Wittman, F.D. (ed.), *The Homeless with Alcohol-Related Problems.* Rockville, MD: U.S. Department of Health and Human Services.

Rothman, D.J. (1971). *The Discovery of the Asylum: Social Order and Disorder in the New Republic*. Boston: Little, Brown & Co.

Sadd, S. (1985). The revolving door revisited: Public inebriates' use of medical and nonmedical detoxification services in New York City. In Wittman, F.D. (ed.), *The Homeless with Alcohol-Related Problems*. Rockville, MD: U.S. Department of Health and Human Services.

Sadd, S. & Young, D.W. (1987). Nonmedical treatment of indigent alcoholics. *Alcohol Health & Research World, 11,* 48–9, 53.

Segal, S.P., Baumohl, J. & Johnson, E. (1977). Falling through the cracks: Mental disorder and social margin in a young vagrant population. *Social Problems, 24,* 387–400.

Segal, S.P. & Baumohl, J. (1980). Engaging the disengaged: Proposals on madness and vagrancy. *Social Work, 25,* 358–65.

Shandler, I.W. & Shipley, T.E. (1987). New focus for an old problem: Philadelphia's response to homelessness. *Alcohol Health & Research World, 11,* 54–7, 91.

Smith, H.W. (1981). *Strategies of social research: The methodological imagination,* 2nd ed. Englewood Cliffs, NJ: Prentice-Hall.

Stark, L. (1987). A century of alcohol and homelessness: Demographics and stereotypes. *Alcohol Health & Research World, 11,* 8–13.

Vaillant, G.E. (1983). *The Natural History of Alcoholism*. Cambridge, MA: Harvard University Press.

Wittman, F.D. (1985). *The Homeless with Alcohol-Related Problems: Proceedings of a Meeting to Provide Research Recommendations to the National Institute on Alcohol Abuse and Alcoholism (NIAAA)*. Rockville, MD: U.S. Department of Health and Human Services.

Wonnacott, R.J. & Wonnacott, T.H. (1970). *Econometrics*. New York: John Wiley.

Wootton, B. (1959). *Social science and social pathology,* London: George Allen and Unwin.

Wright, J.D., Knight, J.W., Weber-Burdin, E. & Lam, J. (1987). Ailments and alcohol: Health status among the drinking homeless. *Alcohol Health & Research World, 11,* 22–6, 89.

8
World Poverty and Homelessness

T hus far we have portrayed homelessness as if it were unique to the United States. However, in less-developed countries (LDCs), homelessness has long been a fact of life. Estimates suggest the problem for LDCs will grow much worse:

> [O]ne billion people [approximately one quarter of the world's population] . . . live in absolute poverty and are either literally homeless or live in extremely inadequate shelters and unhealthy environments. (Munro 1987, p. 5)

Raising people out of poverty in LDCs, while certainly humane and beneficial, poses some costs to the United States. No matter how a particular strategy for international development is implemented, it inevitably requires some redistribution of wealth from a more developed country, such as the United States, to an LDC, such as Sri Lanka. Admittedly, over the long-term, LDCs may become markets for exports from the United States. But over the short-term, developed countries will experience some economic dislocation. This will in turn require standards of living in developed countries to adjust downward. The policies we have suggested in other chapters can prevent this adjustment from occurring disproportionately among the poor. In this chapter, we will review development in LDCs, show how that development impinges on homelessness in the United States, and outline a policy for worldwide growth that does not impinge negatively on either an LDC or a developed country such as the United States.

Third World Development

Several strategies have been used to foster third world development: first, LDCs have taken advantage of the global search for cheap labor and have offered the incentive of little government interference in their countries as opposed to more developed countries; and second, LDCs have abandoned welfare-oriented economies and used loans from developed (core) nations to develop their infrastructures. The first strategy has *directly* resulted in loss of jobs in the United States, and the second has *indirectly* resulted in loss of jobs in the United States.

The first strategy in which LDCs have assisted developed countries in their search for cheap labor began in the late 1950s when U.S. corporations started to realize the difficulty in exploiting cheap labor within its borders (Palloix 1977; Slater 1985). As a result, manufacturing jobs in developed countries began to disappear (Gorz 1983; Massey & Meegan 1982). Harris (1984) estimates that in the 1970s more than 900,000 manufacturing jobs in the United States were eliminated, and by 1982, one out of every four jobs in manufacturing had been eliminated.

Many of these jobs were exported to world market factories, where transnational corporations could more easily exploit cheap labor and take advantage of few government controls (Schiffer 1981). These factories were essentially owned and operated by a foreign national, such as a U.S. firm, in an LDC, such as Sri Lanka, where the products produced were sold in the developed country. In other words, the world market factories did not produce goods for local consumption, and the majority, if not all, of the revenues of the factory went to the foreign national.

LDCs were quick to set up economic incentives, such as restrictions on workers to form trade unions, few or no mandated fringe benefits, credits for foreign investment, and export-free processing zones (Henderson 1986).

There is a great deal of debate about how many U.S. jobs were lost as the result of exporting jobs to LDCs. Some scholars (Bosworth & Lawrence 1988–89) point out that less than one-third of U.S. imports currently come from low-wage countries, as defined as countries with average wages less than half of the U.S. level. In 1960, two-thirds of U.S. imports came from low-wage countries. How can it be argued that U.S. jobs are being exported when U.S. imports from LDCs are low when compared with the 1960s? First, import statistics do not measure profits from U.S. corporations that are made overseas as a result of those corporations selling products that had formerly been produced by U.S. workers, and second, many products sold in the United States as domestically produced have components that are manufactured overseas. Therefore, analysts who use import figures as a measure of U.S. dependence on products from LDCs are underestimating the flight of U.S. jobs overseas. For example, in 1979, the Coca Cola Company made 63 percent of its profits from overseas operations and Ford Motor Company made 94 percent (Bell 1987). Harrison and Bluestone (1988) note that in 1983 many multinational firms received the bulk of their profits from offshore affiliates.

This raises two important points: first, many of the products sold overseas would have been produced in the United States, but are now produced in foreign countries because of cheaper labor and fewer government controls; and second, it is difficult, if not impossible, to determine how many products fit into this category because the U.S. government does not require U.S. corporations to maintain accurate records on job exportation. For example, a corporation may close down a portion of its productive capacity and purchase or develop a similar facility in an LDC; however, there is seldom a connection made between the U.S. jobs lost and the creation of the same job in an LDC. As already noted, 900,000 jobs a year in the mid-1970s were eliminated (Harris 1984). Some of these jobs were transferred overseas—just how many is hard to determine.

In chapter 1 we discussed the deindustrialization of America and the loss of U.S. jobs overseas. The Bureau of Labor Statistics (BLS) observes that ". . . the shift to a service economy is not really evidence of a declining industrial base, or 'deindustrialization'" (Kutscher & Personick 1986, p. 91). Government economists admit that between 1959 and 1984 there was a 12.3 percentage drop in manufacturing jobs. They, as opposed to Harrison and Bluestone, highlight losses in the agricultural sector as opposed to goods-producing sector. Thus, the government admits that manufacturing jobs have been lost, but uses terms such as "relative" and "not declined appreciably" to describe the decline in these manufacturing jobs. The 900,000 jobs lost are therefore "relative" according to the government. As we have already discussed, this depends on your vantage point. Interestingly, the Bureau of Labor Statistics devotes one sentence in its 1986 article on deindustrialization to the hardships caused by job losses. It is precisely this bias that prevents us from citing how many U.S. jobs were exported overseas. For as long as government economists consider job losses relative and not significant, there is little incentive to maintain the kind of data necessary to trace where jobs lost in the United States have gone.

Although we are not able to provide empirical data, there are numerous reports of how U.S. jobs have been exported overseas. For example, during the late 1970s, in particular, studies found that U.S. corporations directed their foreign subsidiaries in LDCs to sell goods (not previously produced in the LDC) to their subsidiaries in high-tax (developed) countries at significantly inflated prices (Braithwaite 1979). This process could not have taken place unless U.S. corporations had exported some jobs from their U.S. plants.

An example of how U.S. corporations have taken advantage of lower overseas wage rates is the production of the Mercury Tracer. Shaiken (1987) notes:

> The car was designed by the Japanese and its engine and transmission will also be built in Japan. The car itself will be assembled in Mexico and sold in the United States. What is important is not just the transfer of the labor-intensive parts of the vehicle's production, but a worldwide division of labor

from the point of design to the point of assembly, wherever both happen to be most convenient for the firm. (p. 47)

In this case, the firm in question is an American firm, Ford Motor Company. If not for the lower wage rates of Mexico, Ford would produce the Tracer in the United States. As a result, manufacturing in the United States declined and some jobs that would have been created here were created overseas, and some U.S. jobs were actually eliminated and exported overseas.

Another example is the rate of growth in manufacturing along the Mexican border. In 1965, the U.S. and Mexican governments entered into an agreement known as the Maquiladora program, in which the infrastructure on the Mexican side of the border was developed. The Maquiladora program encouraged U.S. manufacturing firms to locate in Mexico by offering cheap labor and a policy in which U.S. firms could import, without tariff charges, raw materials into Mexico. As noted by U.S. government economists, the "popularity of this program with U.S. businesses is attributable to the cost advantage of using *less expensive* Mexican labor" (Harrell & Fischer 1985). In 1983, the prevailing wage rate in Mexico for these workers was 90 cents an hour (Turner 1983). By 1983, 594 Maquiladora assembly plants were employing 156,000 workers (Turner 1983). Although this creation of jobs is important for Mexico, there is little doubt that it comes at the expense of jobs for U.S. workers.

The loss of manufacturing jobs, while potentially beneficial to LDCs, has had a negative impact on the U.S. economy. Particularly devastated by the loss of manufacturing jobs are the less-educated, unskilled laborers. Admittedly, the loss of manufacturing jobs has been accompanied by a growth in service-sector jobs. However, we have illustrated how blacks, in particular, have not gained access to these jobs. As a result, unemployment for blacks has skyrocketed from 7.6 percent in 1969 to 30.4 percent in 1985 (McChesney 1989). Not surprisingly, the real unemployment rate in central cities for black men aged 16 to 64 is 51.2 percent (Kasarda 1988). While the loss of manufacturing jobs to LDCs may have paved the way for white collar jobs in the United States that require high levels of education, it has eroded traditional routes of employment for less-educated minority groups.

Scholars such as Harrison and Bluestone (1988) tie this process to the increase in poverty, and we link increased poverty to the rise in homelessness. As noted in chapter 1, this position is contested by conservative analysts, such as Robert Samuelson, who label Harrison and Bluestone's analysis a "big lie" (Levinson 1989). Not surprisingly, conservative analysts use different (lower) levels of inflation to show that wages compare favorably with prices and highlight the high number of part-time jobs to show that lower-paid people are not working full-time. The latter observation about the higher number of part-time jobs may not, as argued by many conservatives, come about because workers choose to enter less than full-time employment. Instead, workers are often confronted with the choice of either working part-time or not working at all.

Who is right? That depends on your vantage point. Most of the analysts that contest Harrison and Bluestone's conclusions are supporting the Reagan recovery. We, on the other hand, show how the Reagan "recovery" benefited primarily the wealthy, punished the poor, and allowed homelessness to grow at an alarming rate.

In addition to exporting U.S. jobs overseas, U.S. corporations have used the low wage rates of LDCs as justification for either abolishing U.S. jobs or demanding wage concessions from U.S. workers. For example, Pittston Coal group in southwest Virginia demanded that its union coal miners accept wage concessions and modernization in which machines would replace workers' jobs (Struck 1989). The company pointed out that one in three mining jobs has disappeared over the last decade as the result of low-wage, foreign competition. The union struck the mine and later the federal courts ruled that Pittston Coal engaged in unfair labor practices.

The loaning of money to LDCs by U.S. banks has also created economic dislocation in this country. Once again, there is not empirical data to support this conclusion because the government does not trace the factors that contribute to a job either being eliminated or not created. In the 1970s, U.S. banks loaned LDCs money in order to enable them to develop their infrastructures. By 1982, however, with Mexico's near bankruptcy, U.S. banks began to seek relief from the U.S. government and the U.S. taxpayer. In 1989, it was estimated that Latin nations owed U.S. banks $395 million dollars. This relief has once again come at the expense of U.S. jobs.

There was little doubt that many of the LDCs would not be able to repay their mounting external debts. However, the unresolved question that was never addressed was whether it would have been wiser to simply provide grants to LDCs instead of using private loans from U.S. banks. The decision to use private loans meant that as U.S. banks took a charge against their profits for bad debts of LDCs, the U.S. tax system, which was becoming increasingly regressive, was used as a means to subsidize both LDCs and U.S. banking interests. Thus in the final analysis, the U.S. taxpayer paid for the third world debt debacle, but the burden fell disproportionately on the middle-class taxpayer. In addition, declining profits in U.S. banks provided them with the opportunity to raise interest rates and squeeze credit. This in turn meant that businesses were confronted with higher operating costs and cut their costs by laying off workers.

We are not arguing that LDCs should be denied resources from more developed countries such as the United States. However, too frequently these subsidies come at the expense of those, such as the displaced worker or the overtaxed lower- or middle-class individual.

Benefits to Less-Developed Countries

Just as there is controversy over whether the restructuring of the U.S. economy has been negative for the U.S. work force, there is also controversy over the benefits of this process for LDCs. Some scholars (Frobel et al. 1980) have argued that the technologies transferred are outmoded, and "deskilled" jobs seldom provide any potential or incentive to improve the skills of peripheral (LDC) labor forces. In addition, these scholars argue that it is difficult to integrate world market factories into local economies (Portes & Walton 1981; Rada 1982). They go on to point out that LDCs become highly dependent on the changing attitudes of developed nations, but they do not develop an economic base of their own.

Other scholars note that LDCs are independent and exert their own nationalist agenda on world market factories, in which the products, wages, and capital of these industries are integrated into the local economy (Wright 1978; Williams 1980). In addition, transnational corporations will find that the prevailing wage rate gradually rises, which in turn raises the living standards of the populations in the LDCs.

Admittedly, this is a trickle-down process, and as a result, ownership patterns have not been directly changed. Nevertheless, LDCs, such as Hong Kong and Singapore, have increased standards of living for some of their populace (Lim & Pang 1982; Henderson 1985). While positive for LDCs, this growth has been shouldered by lowering wage rates in the United States, resulting in a decrease in standards of living here.

While not reviving the overall economy of LDCs, the exporting of U.S. jobs has resulted in marginal improvement in living standards in the LDCs. An important observation needs to be made at this juncture. Unfortunately, the exporting of U.S. jobs overseas has not changed the ownership patterns in LDCs. Instead, multinational corporations have maintained the right of ownership and not shared the wealth gained by their investments in LDCs.

This practice has historically been particularly damaging for LDCs. Unable to exert control over the direction of investment into their countries, and already burdened by weak governments, LDCs have often found their economies deindustrialized. Wallerstein (1972), for example, shows that Poland suffered deindustrialization and became a peripheral country as the result of external investment, a weak internal government, and lack of ownership over the means of production. Instead of a diversified and stable economy developing in which the overall economy expands, an export-dominated economy becomes commonplace, in which peripheralization characterizes the prevailing economic structure (Frank 1972). One of the major inhibitors created by a weak state is that workers are not able to apply political leverage to demand higher wages and thus leverage a greater sharing of both wealth and control from the multinational corporations (Shorter & Tilly 1974).

El Salvador provides a graphic example of how a weak state structure combined with foreign investment leads to deteriorating standards of living for the poor. The coffee-growing elite of El Salvador expanded their control of capital-intensive industries during the 1960s and 1970s (Booth 1984). Of the total foreign investment, 80 percent was concentrated in the coffee industry. El Salvador as a country did not benefit from this investment. Instead, unemployment rose, wealth became increasingly concentrated among the coffee barons, and poverty increased dramatically.

A strong state structure and limited foreign investment, however, enabled England and the Netherlands to maintain their economic stability and the people, for the most part, to enjoy greater prosperity (Rubinson 1984). Therefore, from a dependency analysis standpoint, it is the state that must control the investments of foreign national corporations, which are generally firms from developed countries such as the United States. Otherwise, the multinational corporations, such as Ford Motor Company, will make a few local citizens wealthy, but divert most of the wealth they earn away from the country. Critics argue that multinational corporations that create wealth for a host country generally do not analyze the concentration of this wealth (Bauer & Yamey 1975). If, as in countries such as El Salvador, the wealth is concentrated in the hands of the few, the infrastructure of the country deteriorates, and there is no economic mainstream in which the general populace can benefit.

The second means by which LDCs have attempted to raise living standards is by moving away from welfare-oriented economies to market-oriented economies. In order to finance the infrastructure necessary to sustain a market-economy, LDCs borrow heavily from external lenders. Not surprisingly, as LDCs use a process of external debt to develop their infrastructures, there is, at least initially, a significant gap created between rich and poor in which the poor become poorer (Kuznets 1972).

As an example, the case of Sri Lanka is not unusual. In order to develop its infrastructure, Sri Lanka diverted national spending away from welfare programs and toward investments in plants and equipment. At the same time, government controls were lifted, and some industries, such as Air Lanka, received significant government subsidies (Sahn 1987). Meanwhile, the balance of payments became negative because the economy was not yet able to recoup the outflow of capital necessary to repay the increasing foreign debt burden. As Sahn (1987) notes, the reaction of the government was not surprising:

> In response to the high rates of inflation and the growing budget deficits, further austerity measures were adopted in 1980–81, which curtailed some of the economic expansion. This further imperiled those in the lower expenditure deciles. (p. 286)

As already noted, the case of Sri Lanka is the rule, not the exception, when underdeveloped nations attempt to develop infrastructures with foreign capital. Generally, the debt plus the interest payments is much more than the economy is able to generate. For example, $30 billion in capital was drained from Latin American countries to repay principle plus interest to creditor nations during 1986 (Palley 1987). The International Monetary Fund (IMF) has thus far been unsympathetic to the burdens further austerity measures create on debtor nations. In Brazil, for example, approximately 4 percent of economic output is used to service debt (Rowe 1985), while there exist massive slums in Rio de Janeiro and Sao Paulo.

Attempts by LDCs to become active participants in the world economy have thus far failed, in part because the process of development favors already developed nations. As a result, LDCs are dependent on handouts from developed nations. Not wanting to upset the balance of power, developed nations generally strive to maintain the upper hand in all dealings with LDCs. Irving Kristol, a leading conservative thinker, observes: "Nor will the United States really have any alternative but to use such power to recreate a world order it can live with—a world in which there is relatively free trade and relatively free access to resources" (Alperovitz & Faux 1984, p. 67). This statement underscores a belief held by many Americans that the resources of the world are actually the property of the United States, and efforts by LDCs to capitalize on their own resources are perceived as a threat to the ability of developed nations to maintain their own standards of living. In effect, first world nations practice economics of development in third world nations as long as it benefits the interests of developed countries.

Reaction by Less-Developed Countries

The difficulty faced by LDCs as a result of their increasing external debts led to a revolt by President Alan Garcia of Peru in 1985. Garcia declared:

> In the dialogue with our creditors we shall not accept as a precondition the mortgaging of our sovereign independence nor the imposition of internal political conditions through the signing of letters of intent with negative terms for our people. (Garcia 1985)

President Garcia announced a financial moratorium in which Peru would pay no more than 10 percent of its export earnings to service its external debt (Graham 1989). By mid-1987, Garcia's efforts to shield the Peruvian economy from painful austerity measures resulted in a significant downturn in the economy. As a result, Peru faced increasing difficulty in servicing its mounting external debt. In addition, Peru faced a shortage of cash as well as credit to maintain the flow of its economy. Rather than force the poor to bear the main burden of any economic austerity measures, President Garcia demanded economic adjustments from the entrepreneurial classes.

Some scholars (Graham 1989) have criticized Garcia's behavior:

> The president's insistence on watering down difficult economic adjustment measures—and his continued refusal to negotiate with Peru's international creditors—has devastated the economy and helped to polarize the political system. (p. 47)

The foregoing analysis overlooks the fact that economic adjustment measures are generally reserved for the poor, and the entrepreneurial classes are able to evade taxation by either investment overseas or through a domestic tax system that is inherently regressive. As a result, when LDCs go looking for ways to reduce the share of their budgets devoted to domestic programs and increase the share of their budgets that service their foreign debts, they reduce government subsidies for the poor and other welfare programs. The ability of the poor to purchase food and other necessities is greatly reduced.

Rather than have LDCs redistribute domestic wealth, the United States has long supported foreign governments that uphold the values of private property. Former President Salvador Allende of Chile challenged the notion that private property and a free enterprise system was the best way of creating economic stability. Today the affluent in Chile are enjoying economic prosperity; however, the income gap between rich and poor continues to worsen. In many ways, Chile has followed the suggestions of the International Monetary Fund (IMF) and implemented a severe austerity program in which living standards for the poor have deteriorated. Those countries, such as Chile, face U.S. sanctions when attempting a different course in which domestic wealth is redistributed and U.S. corporations' assets are nationalized.

Fear of countries that attempt to support labor movements shows the historic U.S. tunnel vision toward economic systems that in some way deviate from capitalism (Cantor & Schor 1987). Such fear also points out the favoritism capital enjoys in the United States over workers.

An exception to this is Costa Rica, where a social democratic political style of government has maintained a small military and has redistributed wealth. Unlike their Latin neighbors El Salvador and Nicaragua, before the revolution, Costa Rica had engaged in an aggressive land reform program that redistributed land to peasants (Seligson 1980). Thus far, although not receiving significant U.S. aid, Costa Rica has not been punished for their foray into noncapitalistic methods. It should be noted, however, that although Costa Rica has made progress in addressing the needs of its poorest citizens, it still remains an LDC in search of a means of entering the world economy.

Clearly, the present process of international development is not benefiting either the poor in the LDCs or the average U.S. worker. The winners in the current international division of labor are U.S. corporations that can take advantage of cheap foreign labor, fewer government controls, and evade U.S. taxation. For example, in 1981, overseas tax shelters enabled U.S. corporations with profits between $1.1 billion and $9.6 billion to receive tax refunds or owe no taxes (Bell 1987, p. 81). LDCs, such as Mexico, have aided this process by adopting austerity measures designed to enable them to repay loans to U.S. banks and also keep their citizens willing to work for desperately low wages.

In order for LDCs to compete equally in the world market with developed nations, a change in the world balance of power is necessary. As long as developed nations maintain their privileged status in the global economy, LDCs will remain dependent and poor.

Economic Improvement for Less-Developed Countries and Prevention of Homelessness in the United States

The Sixth Special Session of the General Assembly of the United Nations endorsed the following ideas to improve standards of living in LDCs: transferring economic, technological, and informational resources; allowing for more decision making by LDCs in the world monetary system; paying higher prices for raw materials exported from LDCs to developed nations; and sharing control of foreign firms in LDCs (Sharma & Rubin 1984). These proposals in one way or another require developed nations to share some of their wealth with LDCs. Given the fact that much of this wealth, for example profits obtained by exploiting labor from LDCs, was obtained in a less than equitable manner from LDCs, some sharing of wealth seems appropriate.

It is doubtful that LDCs will be able to purchase expensive advanced technologies by selling their cheaper-priced raw materials. Therefore, some global redistribution of wealth is necessary to achieve global prosperity. Our concern is that wealth be redistributed from those who can afford it and that the poor in the United States are not used as a means to achieve these ends.

This can be achieved in the following ways: first, reduce the tax shelters available to multinational corporations that invest overseas; second, require that investments made by multinational corporations overseas be jointly owned by both the foreign country and the corporation; third, export technologies to LDCs through an arrangement by which the purchase price is, in lieu of cash, the requirement that the LDCs agree to use the technology for peaceful means; fourth, forgive much of the debt owed by LDCs; fifth, keep track of jobs exported overseas and of products that are partially produced overseas; sixth, offer free technical advice to LDCs interested in developing their countries; seventh, add a 5 percent tax increase to upper incomes and corporations in order to provide grants, not loans, to LDCs; and eighth, develop a foreign policy that rewards nation states such as Costa Rica and penalizes those such as El Salvador.

Reduce Tax Shelters

The first issue is to greatly reduce the tax shelters enjoyed by U.S. firms that invest overseas. Not only does this reduce revenue to the U.S. Treasury and place a greater burden on the individual taxpayer, but it also means that many U.S. corporations evade taxation all together. Critics will immediately charge that this will act as a disincentive for overseas investment. However, we have already shown that this type of investment is harmful both to the United States and to the LDC. While these investments may marginally raise standards of living in LDCs, they do not transfer ownership of needed technology or control of the means of production. In addition, the U.S. economy suffers because jobs are exported overseas and U.S. workers are displaced.

Less-Developed Countries as Joint Owners

Instead of the current model in which multinational corporations do not share the wealth created by their investment with the LDC, new laws need to be passed in which U.S. firms that do business overseas are required to enter into joint ventures (50–50 split of ownership) with LDCs. In order to ensure that the multinational corporations perform as mandated by law, they would be required to file reports of their activities to a United Nations commission and face a significant (100 percent) penalty on all earnings if they failed to comply. Is the United Nations the best forum for this process? Although the United Nations has been ineffective in some arenas, such as when it condemns a specific action by a government, some of their peace-keeping duties have met with more success. Important for this process to work is to generate the support of the superpowers. Otherwise, multinational corporations and foreign governments may ignore decisions by the United Nations.

Export Technologies

One of the greatest barriers confronted by LDCs is that the technology needed to upgrade their infrastructures is prohibitively expensive and is often not sold by developed countries. As is more often the case, a multinational corporation will employ a particular technology in an LDC, but it will not share the actual technology with the LDC. Part of this problem will be remedied by the requirement that all U.S. multinational corporations enter into joint ventures with LDCs. However, there will remain the problem of LDCs needing technology and being unable to afford it or being denied access to it. Except in the case of technology needed for defense, such as a particular design that enhances the ability of a jet fighter to spot targets at night, other technologies can be safely exported without fear of them being used in a hostile manner against the United States.

On the other hand, critics will charge that the sharing of technology will diminish the ability of the United States to compete. This is not completely true. Japan uses much the same technology to produce cars as does the United States. However, it is not technology that provides Japan with an advantage in the automobile market. Much of Japan's success has to do with their employment system, which envisions the worker as a human being with needs instead of an expense item, as in the United States, that has to be managed properly. In Japan, for example, there is less antagonism between workers and management because the corporation is seen as a community that respects and looks after its workers. This philosophy reduces worker turnover and raises morale. It has been estimated that efforts to reduce worker turnover in the U.S. workplace would raise productivity by 30 percent or more and increase profits (Vogel 1979). Therefore, the sharing of technology will simply mean that the U.S. corporation will have to become more creative and abandon outdated methods of operation that are based on the notion that workers are expendable.

Debt Forgiveness

Any approach to improve the economies of LDCs has to eliminate the burdensome debts owed to developed countries. Otherwise, any wealth created by new forms of ownership will be siphoned off to repay external debts. Thus far, most plans to address the debt problem have favored banks in developed countries by insisting that the debt be maintained, but the terms of the debt repayment be somehow rescheduled. This approach ignores the practices of multinational corporations that continue to reap profits in LDCs, but pay little if any taxes to the LDC.

Therefore, rather than perpetuate the myth that the foreign debts owed by LDCs will ever be repaid, we argue that these debts be forgiven and a system of grants be set up to finance future development in LDCs. Obviously, such a large loss could not be sustained by the U.S. banking system without creating an economic downturn. Therefore, a relevant question for discussion is whether the U.S. Treasury should bail out the banking system, and if so, by how much.

Someone will have to pay for this bail-out—should it be the owners of the banks, the U.S. taxpayer, or the U.S. worker in the form of tighter credit and higher interest rates? The best approach is the one that creates the least disruption in the economy. Therefore, we favor an approach that requires banks to charge off a portion of the third world debt each year. However, the tax laws would be amended so as not allow the banks to reduce their income tax liability by the amount of debt written off. Obviously, banks will pass along the cost of these losses to bank customers in the form of higher charges. In addition, banks will probably tighten credit in order to justify higher interest rates. At this point, the federal government will have to intervene by monitoring interest rates in conjunction with the Federal Reserve to ensure that banks do not take advantage of the situation.

Critics will be quick to point out that this will unfairly penalize banks. Therefore, the federal government should allow banks to take a one-time charge against current income and deduct it from their tax liability. This one-time charge would be calculated for each bank, would take into account the vulnerability of individual banks, and would determine how much austerity these banks will have to bear. Of particular concern would be to disallow a bank to take a charge against current income and then turn around and give their top management substantial raises.

Tracking Exportation of Jobs and Products

All the approaches discussed thus far would be of negligible benefit to the United States and to LDCs unless legislation were passed that monitored jobs exported overseas by U.S. corporations. This would require U.S. corporations to maintain records that keep track of jobs eliminated in the United States, jobs created overseas, and any profits from overseas investments. Failure to comply with this legislation would be taken seriously and would result in direct seizure of a corporation's assets. This approach would enable the government to keep track of how many jobs were being lost to cheap overseas labor and enable LDCs to monitor when multinational corporations were expanding their investments in LDCs.

Technical Advice

Our next approach to help LDCs develop their economies is to provide them with free technical advice. This can be done in a way that costs the American taxpayer relatively little. University students in different professions could receive free tuition if they agreed to a specified number of years of service in an LDC. This approach would enable students to gain valuable experience overseas and help impoverished countries to gain access to technology that would otherwise be prohibitively expensive.

Raising Tax Rates and Providing Grants

The most controversial of our suggestions is the notion that the federal tax system should be used to create a pool of money that would be given to LDCs in the form of grants as opposed to loans. The use of loans to LDCs is similar to when coal operators in the 19th century operated a company store in which the miners bought goods and services at inflated prices with subsistence wages. Much like the miners who never escaped debt, LDCs have found that loans only make matters worse. Grants, on the other hand, are given to an LDC without repayment obligations. As a result, profits from development would become part of the wealth of an LDC. Progressive taxes can provide the revenues to underwrite this program.

Foreign Policy that Rewards Countries

Finally, we urge the creation of a foreign policy that supports countries, such as Costa Rica, that are actively trying to improve the lives of *all* their citizens. This approach is much different than current efforts that reward countries, such as Chile or El Salvador, that favor affluence for the wealthy at the expense of the poor. The specifics of this policy include stopping loans or aid to nations such as El Salvador and Chile. It is ironic that our government has chosen to support foreign governments that are nothing more than dictatorships in which a wealthy elite class holds power.

Concluding Remarks

World poverty did not come about because of the inherent deficiencies of individual countries. Instead, world poverty, much like homelessness in the United States, was created to enable some individuals within developed nations to enjoy higher standards of living. As suggested by some conservatives and liberals, the United States can either go to war or enact reactive trade policy as a means of addressing this crisis. On the other hand, resources from this nation can be redistributed to LDCs.

Inevitably, this will require many Americans, not just the wealthy and large corporations, to make permanent changes in their lifestyles. For example, coffee may cost more because Latin American countries may begin to exact a higher price for their products. This in turn will mean that Americans, in general, will have to pay higher prices.

Much like the discussions in other chapters in this book, efforts to redress the mistakes of the past and eliminate poverty and homelessness require people to make choices. There is no inexpensive way to address this problem. Important questions for consideration are:

- Will the cost be shared by all in a progressive manner or will the cost fall disproportionately on the poor?
- Will Americans decide that the resources of the LDCs are rightfully ours and use force to get them?

At the center of any effort to help the homeless, whether it is in the United States or in a foreign country, is the willingness to address historic inequities that currently maintain poverty. Much as we have argued in the other chapters of this book, any economic system that favors the affluent over the poor will create some homelessness. Therefore, the reduction of world poverty must be linked to a global economic system that seeks to create an economic balance so that the poor, through their low wages, will not be subsidizing a higher lifestyle for the affluent.

The fortunes of the United States are directly linked to the fortunes of other countries. The reverse is also true. We are particularly concerned that the continued quest for prosperity by the United States as well as other countries does not come at the expense of poor people in any country. In the final analysis, efforts to help the homeless must assume a global stance that attempts to equalize resources worldwide.

References

Alperovitz, G. & Faux, J. (1984). *Rebuilding America.* New York: Pantheon Books.

Bauer, P.T. & Yamey, B.S. (1957). *The Economics of Underdeveloped Nations.* Chicago: University of Chicago Press.

Bell, W. (1987). *Contemporary Social Welfare.* New York: Macmillan.

Booth, J.A. (1984). "Trickle-up" income redistribution and development in Central America during the 1960s and 1970s. In Seligson, M.A. (ed.), *The Gap Between Rich and Poor: Contending Perspectives on the Political Economy of Development.* London: Westview Press, 351–65.

Bosworth, B. & Lawrence, R.Z. (1988–89). America in the world economy. *The Brookings Review, 7,* (1): 39–48.

Braithwaite, J. (1979). Crime and the abuse of power in international perspective. In *Report of the Interregional Meeting of Experts on Crime and the Abuse of Power: Offenses and Offenders Beyond the Reach of the Law.* New York: United Nations, July 9–13, 22–3.

Cantor, D. & Schor, J. (1987). *Tunnel Vision: Labor, the World Economy, and Central America.* Boston: South End Press.

Frank, A.G. (1972). The development of underdevelopment. In Cockcroft, J.D., Frank, A.G. & Johnson, D. (eds.), *Dependence and Underdevelopment.* New York: Doubleday.

Frobel, F., Henrichs, J. & Kreye, O. (1980). *The New International Division of Labour.* Cambridge, UK: Cambridge University Press.

Garcia, A.P. (1985). Address, provisional transcript, United Nations General Assembly, 40th session, A/40/PV.5/. New York: United Nations, September 25.

Gorz, A. (1983). *Farewell to the Working Class.* London: Pluto Press.

Graham, C.L. (1989). The Latin American quagmire. *The Brookings Review, 7,* (2): 42–7.

Harrell, L. & Fischer, D. (1985). The 1982 Mexican peso devaluation and border area employment. *Monthly Labor Review, 108,* (10): 25–32.

Harris, C.S. (1984). The magnitude of job loss from plant closings and the generation of replacement jobs: Some recent evidence. *Annals of the American Academy of Political and Social Science,* September, 475.

Harrison, B. & Bluestone, B. (1988). *The Great U-Turn: Corporate Restructuring and the Polarizing of America.* New York: Basic Books, Inc.

Henderson, J. (1985). The new international division of labour and American semiconductor production in South-East Asia. In Dixon, C., Drakakis-Smith, D. & Watts, D. (eds.), *Multinational Companies and the Third World.* London: Croom Helm.

Henderson, J. (1986). The new international division of labour and urban development in the world system. In Drakakis-Smith, D. (ed.), *Urbanization in the Developing World*. Dover, N.H.: Croom Helm, 63–82.

Kasarda, J.D. (1988). Jobs, migration, and emerging urban mismatches. In McGeary, M.G.H. & Lynn, L.E. Jr. (eds.), *Urban Change and Poverty*. Washington, D.C: National Academy Press, 148–98.

Kutscher, R.E. & Personick, V.A. (1986). Deindustrialization and the shift to services. *Monthly Labor Review, 109,* (6): 3–13.

Kuznets, S. (1972). *Economic Growth of Nations*. Cambridge, MA: Harvard University Press.

Levinson, M. (1989). Some truth about our economy. *Dissent,* Spring, 277–79.

Lim, L.Y.C. & Pang, E.F. (1982). Vertical linkages and multinational enterprises in developing countries. *World Development, 10,* (7): 585–95.

Massey, D. & Meegan, R. (1982). *The Anatomy of Job Loss*. London: Methuen.

McChesney, K.Y. (1989). Macroeconomic issues in poverty: Implications for child and youth homelessness. Presented at "Homeless Children and Youth: Coping with a National Tragedy." Washington, D.C.: April 25–29.

Munro, I. (1987). International year of shelter for the homeless. *Cities, 4,* (1): 5–12.

Palley, H.A. (1987). The debt crisis: An examination of pressures and strains in the Americas. *International Journal of Contemporary Sociology, 24,* (3–4): 15–16.

Palloix, C. (1977). The self explanation of capital on a world scale. *Review of Radical Political Economics, 9,* (2): 1–28.

Perez, A.G. (1985). Address. Provisional Transcript United Nations General Assembly, 40th Session, A/40/PV.5. New York: United Nations, September 23.

Portes, A. & Walton, J. (1981). *Labor, Class, and the International System*. New York: Academic Press.

Rada, J. (1982). *The Structure and Behavior of the Semiconductor Industry*. Geneva: U.N. Center for Transnational Corporations.

Rowe, J.L. Jr. (1985). Brazil looks forward to the past. *The Washington Post National Weekly Edition,* October 7, 17.

Rubinson, R. (1984). The world-economy and the distribution of income within states: A cross-national study. In Seligson, M.A. (ed.), *The Gap Between Rich and Poor—Contending Perspectives on the Political Economy of Development*. London: Westview Press.

Sahn, D.E. (1987). Changes in the living standards of the poor in Sri Lanka during a period of macroeconomic restructuring. *World Development, 15,* (6): 809–30.

Schiffer, J. (1981). The changing post-war pattern of development: The accumulated wisdom of Samir Amin. *World Development, 9,* (6), 515–37.

Seligson, M.A. (1980). *Peasants of Costa Rica and the Development of Agrarian Capitalism*. Madison, WI: University of Wisconsin Press.

Shaiken, H. (1987). Globalization and the worldwide division of labor. *Monthly Labor Review, 110,* (8): 47.

Sharma, S. & Rubin G.K. (1984). New international order: Some premises and bases of social welfare in the third world nations. *Social Development Issues, 8,* (Spring/Summer): 129.

Shorter, E. & Tilly, C. (1974). *Strikes in France, 1830–1968*. Cambridge, UK: Cambridge University Press.

Slater, D. (1985). *Territory and State in Latin America.* London: Macmillan.

Struck, D. (1989). Tensions growing in Va. coal strike. *The Baltimore Sun, 304,* (154): A1.

Turner, R. (1983). Mexico turns in its in-bond industry as a means of generating exchange. *Business America,* November 28, 2.

Vogel, E. (1979). *Japan as Number One.* Cambridge, MA: Harvard University Press, 82–3.

Wallerstein, I. (1972). Three paths of national development in the 16th century. *Studies in Comparative International Development, 8,* 95–101.

Williams, R. (1980). Base and superstructure in Marxist cultural theory. In Williams, R. (ed.), *Problems in Materialism and Culture.* London: Verso, 31–49.

Wright, E.O. (1978). *Class, Crisis, and the State.* London: New Left Books.

Index

About the Authors

John R. Belcher has a Masters in Social Work from the University of Kentucky, a Masters in Divinity from Lexington Theological Seminary, and a Ph.D. in Social Work from Ohio State University. He is an assistant professor at the University of Maryland. Prior to his career in academia, he worked as a therapist with the chronically mentally ill. His current interests focus on addressing the changing economic landscape in America and finding improved methods of addressing poverty. Dr. Belcher is married and has a son.

Frederick A. DiBlasio has a Masters in Social Work from the University of Maryland and a Ph.D. in Social Work and Social Policy from Virginia Commonwealth University. He is an assistant professor at the University of Maryland; formerly, he was an assistant professor at Virginia Commonwealth University. Prior to his academic appointments, he practiced as a social worker providing family, group, and individual therapy at in- and outpatient treatment centers. His current interests include homelessness, effects of poverty on children and families, and adolescent issues. Dr. DiBlasio is married and has three children.